I0801640

Praise for

LEADING THROUGH SPIRALS OF INQUIRY: FOR EQUITY AND QUALITY

If *Leading Through Spirals of Inquiry* were required reading for every education leader, school systems and the world would be a much better place. Judy Halbert and Linda Kaser invite readers to journey with them as they examine how adults can help every child "cross the stage with dignity, purpose, and options." This book is at once a practical guide for school personnel and a manifesto on how to transform, and leapfrog forward, our education systems.

—Rebecca Winthrop, Senior Fellow and Co-Director, Center for Universal Education, The Brookings Institution

The chapters in *Leading Through Spirals of Inquiry* provide a pathway towards implementing a cycle of inquiry that makes a significant difference to students and to the collective purpose of schools. Judy Halbert and Linda Kaser's framework challenges us to move slowly through a process of curiosity and inquiry to create a culture of learning that continually asks us to consider what matters most to student learning, and more importantly, how we know.

—Rosa Fazio, Principal, Sir Sandford Fleming Elementary School

Judy Halbert and Linda Kaser approach teaching and learning with the respect and wisdom it deserves. Every part of this book acknowledges the complexity of education, but cuts through it to offer practical ways to keep being and doing better. If you want to make a real difference for children and young people, this book is where to start. I know I will be carrying it with me for a long time to come.

—Dr. Amelia Peterson, Associate Professor, London Interdisciplinary School, England

Judy Halbert and Linda Kaser's Spiral of Inquiry framework reflects the importance of relationships, curiosity, trust, examination of biases and assumptions, and high expectations of both learners and ourselves. Embedded in this work is the understanding that Indigenous knowledge systems have positive impacts on learning environments, and that quality education systems require equity for Indigenous learners. I look forward to more educators engaging in this powerful and accessible inquiry process for the benefit of both learners and our larger society.
***—Jo Chrona, Author of* Wayi Wah! Indigenous Pedagogies: An Act for Reconciliation and Anti-Racist Education**

Leading Through Spirals of Inquiry is simultaneously friendly and deeply challenging. I felt the easy warmth of the book but not for a moment did I feel complacent. The profound link between the lifetime work of the authors and their deep integration with Indigenous ways of thinking and action greatly expands the agenda before us. Judy Halbert and Linda Kaser first invite and then compel us to take action, while providing the tools for achieving impact on a large scale.
—Michael Fullan, Professor Emeritus, OISE/University of Toronto

Through their humility, experience, wisdom, and passion, Judy Halbert and Linda Kaser provide a way forward for educators in our quest to support greater equity and quality in schools and education systems. *Leading Through Spirals of Inquiry* will compel readers to connect, collaborate, and intentionally create a preferred future for the young people we serve.
—Suzanne Hoffman, CEO, BC School Trustees Association

The phrase "connecting research to practice for equity" is often used to describe work that fails to make explicit the meaningful connection between the work of scholars and the lives of practitioners. *Leading Through Spirals of Inquiry* is a rare exception. This book comes to life with accessible prose that delivers complex ideas grounded in evidence and equity-minded practices that have the potential to transform and restore educational communities.
—Alan J. Daly, Professor and Director of Leadership Doctoral Programs, University of California, San Diego

Leading Through Spirals of Inquiry should be within arm's reach of any educator who wants to transform their classroom, school, or district for the better. The authors' simple yet powerful step-by-step approach to improving teaching and learning for *all* is laden with accessible microbites of research that truly make sense. This, mixed with authentic stories, draws you in and leaves you more curious about your learners than when you first cracked the cover.
—Barb Hamblett, Principal, Valleyview Secondary School

The power of networks and networking has been described as the "New Power." Judy Halbert and Linda Kaser and their now global Networks of Inquiry and Indigenous Education have been exercising this power for sufficient time to know the impact of inquiry leadership teams transforming the learning of young people. Their networks of leaders activate the equity/quality dynamic for all learners. This book reveals what real learning transformation looks like. It conveys, at once, compelling evidence, inspirational practice, and the shared consciousness of the pursuit of powerful purpose.
—Anthony Mackay, CEO, National Center on Education and the Economy

In *Leading Through Spirals of Inquiry*, Judy Halbert and Linda Kaser brilliantly synthesize over twenty years of learning, experience, networking, and wisdom. They provide clear steps educational leaders can take to create more powerful learning and equity in their school communities. Every person leading educational transformation, whether they are new to the Spirals of Inquiry framework or looking to go deeper, should have a copy of this book on their desk.
—Jim Laird, Principal, Canyon Falls Middle School

Leading Through Spirals of Inquiry is a goldmine for everyone in the field of education, no matter where you are working or what your position. If your goal is to make sure our young citizens get the best start possible, every page in this thought-provoking book will encourage and support you, providing a foundation for personal reflection and professional dialogue. Congratulations, my friend—you are about to read a great book that will give you hope and strength as you bravely continue your work as a leader in education.
—Lillemor Rehnberg, Retired Principal and Principal Educator, Sweden

Judy Halbert and Linda Kaser hold a mirror up to our highest and best selves, prompting us to map a collective path toward a future where every child is seen, loved, and thriving. To prepare us for this journey, they provide astute guideposts, powerful questions for reflection, and a broad research base. This book is a perseverance of hope written by two educators who have seen reason to remain certain about the power of educators to change the world.

—Brooke Moore, District Principal of Inquiry and Innovation, Delta School District

In the world of professional learning and educational change, it is rare to find a resource both completely grounded in the real-life practice of educators and steeped in current and seminal research. Judy Halbert and Linda Kaser's voices of experience and those of many other educators are woven among important western and Indigenous perspectives, resulting in a potent guide for those wishing to catalyze quality learning and equity.

—Wendy Carr, Professor of Teaching Emerita, University of British Columbia

LEADING THROUGH SPIRALS OF INQUIRY

JUDY HALBERT AND LINDA KASER

LEADING THROUGH SPIRALS OF INQUIRY

For Equity and Quality

PORTAGE & MAIN PRESS

Portage & Main Press gratefully acknowledges the financial support of the Province of Manitoba through the Department of Sport, Culture and Heritage and the Manitoba Book Publishing Tax Credit, and the Government of Canada through the Canada Book Fund (CBF) for our publishing activities.

Printed and bound in Canada by Friesens.
Front cover design by Frank Reimer
Interior and back cover design by Jennifer Lum

Library and Archives Canada Cataloguing in Publication
Title: Leading through spirals of inquiry : for equity and quality / Judy Halbert, Linda Kaser.
Names: Halbert, Judy, 1949- author. | Kaser, Linda, author.
Description: Includes bibliographical references.
Identifiers: Canadiana (print) 2022018819X | Canadiana (ebook) 20220188408
ISBN 9781774920206 (softcover) | ISBN 9781774920282 (EPUB) ISBN 9781774920275 (PDF)
Subjects: LCSH: Learning. | LCSH: School environment. | LCSH: Effective teaching.
LCSH: Educational leadership. | LCSH: Inclusive education. | LCSH: Career development.
Classification: LCC LB1060 .H35 2022 | DDC 370.15/23—dc23

25 24 23 22 1 2 3 4 5

FSC
www.fsc.org
MIX
Paper from responsible sources
FSC® C016245

ENVIRONMENTAL BENEFITS STATEMENT

Portage & Main Press saved the following resources by printing the pages of this book on chlorine free paper made with 30% post-consumer waste.

TREES	WATER	ENERGY	SOLID WASTE	GREENHOUSE GASES
34 FULLY GROWN	2,700 GALLONS	15 MILLION BTUs	110 POUNDS	14,800 POUNDS

Environmental impact estimates were made using the Environmental Paper Network Paper Calculator 4.0. For more information visit www.papercalculator.org

PORTAGE & MAIN PRESS
www.portageandmainpress.com
Winnipeg, Manitoba
Treaty 1 Territory and homeland of the Métis Nation

For inquiry-minded networked educators everywhere

TABLE OF CONTENTS

INTRODUCTION

WE HOPE YOU are reading this book because you are curious about how to create greater equity and quality in your school and community. You may be a classroom teacher, a formal leader, a system-level leader, a member of the support staff, a teacher candidate, a student leader, a cultural worker, or an interested family member. You may live and work in a complex urban setting or a small rural community. You may be early in your career, or you may be contemplating what your plans might be after your formal career is over. We hope that you have a friend with whom you can share these ideas. Regardless of whether you are reading this on your own or as part of a learning team, you care deeply about the learners in your community, and you want to improve their lives and their life chances.

Throughout this book you will see us refer to inquiry leadership teams. Meeting the complex needs of every learner, and leapfrogging inequality as a system, is impossible for any one teacher, formal leader, or school to do alone. We need to reach out to colleagues for support, encouragement, and challenge. We need to stretch our thinking and question our own assumptions and practices. It is through teamwork that we will grow as professionals and make the greatest difference for our learners.

We believe that leadership is defined more by contribution than by formal title or role. In our view you are a leader if you are willing to step outside of the confines of your own classroom, school, or community to consider the ways in which your actions can contribute to better outcomes for your learners. Yet we also know that the active involvement and support of a formal leader is crucial in maximizing impact.[1] In the chapters to come, we will discuss the roles and opportunities of all leaders, whether informal or formal.

Initially the inquiry leadership team may just be a few individuals committed to system change. In some settings it is a teacher-leader who provides the ongoing leadership. Regardless of the makeup of the group, it is the commitment of the individuals working as a team that will make the difference. When teams meet across schools—in a network—they can have an impact on individual schools and on the system as a whole. Whatever form your own team takes, we hope that you will find ideas, strategies, and examples in the following pages that will deepen and strengthen your work.

This book is a labour of love for us. We have both been in education for a long time. Linda claims she has been in education for her lifetime since, when she was a very young child, her mother ran a kindergarten in their home. She spent her spare time as an elementary school student stapling and filing papers for her father, who was then the president of the local teachers' association. Teaching and activism are in her blood. Judy doesn't have quite as strong a claim for her educational lineage, but with a grandmother and a brother as teachers, it is definitely in her DNA.

We first met when Linda was working for the Ministry of Education for the Province of British Columbia (BC) and came to visit the school where Judy was working as a school counsellor. Judy had developed a group counselling program for students whose families were experiencing separation and divorce. As Linda was looking at the poster on the bulletin board offering a number of different group counselling options, she bumped into Judy. She asked her who had thought up this approach and how it was going. This was a pivotal moment for Judy. Having someone in an important position (like the one Linda had) ask her about her thinking and her practice was unusual. It made her think about the power of a good question and the importance of respectful listening.

Around this time, Linda was known in BC as the "writing lady" for her work in developing a highly successful provincial young writers network. This network brought together teachers from across the province who developed some great strategies, and collectively this network was able to boost writing performance across the grades.

A decade later, Judy was serving as a secondary principal and was working hard to create a more responsive, engaging setting for her learners. She was thriving in this role. At the same time, Linda was asked to move from the elementary school where she was a highly regarded principal to take on the leadership of a very dispirited secondary school.

There were relatively few female principals of large secondary schools in the early '90s, and Linda reached out to Judy for friendship and support. We ended up gathering a small group of female principals who met monthly to exchange ideas, resources, and stories and to enjoy the occasional glass of wine.

THE NETWORK BEGINS

Fast-forward to the summer of 1999 when we were both invited to a meeting that would change the course of our careers for the next two decades. The Ministry of Education had just released a series of learning progressions (BC performance standards) for reading, writing, numeracy, and social responsibility. Hundreds of teachers had been involved in the development of these progressions, and they had the potential to be an invaluable set of resources. The wise person leading this work at the Ministry knew that if the resources were simply sent out to schools in shrink-wrapped binders, the chances of their being widely used were slim to none.

At the meeting, each of us was offered a small grant to see what we could do to encourage teachers to use the materials. It didn't take long for us to decide to consolidate our two regional grants. We knew from our own experience that we needed to involve teams of teachers and principals, that the work needed to be invitational and inquiry-based, and that the meeting structures needed to be simple. This was the starting point for what was originally called the Network of Performance Based Schools.[2] Neither of us would ever have imagined that what started as a simple invitation would become the heart and soul of our lifework.

The network grew steadily over the next ten years and took a big step forward in 2009 when the late and much respected Kwakiutl educator Dr. Trish Rosborough (at that time the Director of Aboriginal Education at the Ministry of Education) asked us to meet with her at a downtown hotel. At the time, the Ministry was encouraging school districts and local Indigenous communities to develop plans to improve the experiences of Indigenous learners. These

Aboriginal Enhancement Agreements required an enormous amount of work at the district and community levels. Collaboratively developed and endorsed, they represented new forms of partnership aimed at creating better experiences for Indigenous learners in BC public schools.

Over a coffee, Trish told us that she had seen that we were having success in developing networks focused on changing outcomes for learners in the key areas of the performance standards. She wondered if we might be willing to develop a similar network focused on Indigenous education. Could we move the goals of the enhancement agreements from being well-intentioned words on paper into action in classrooms? With that invitation and challenge, the Aboriginal Enhancement Schools Network was formed. The response from BC educators to the opportunity to learn more about Indigenous ways of knowing and to change practices to better reflect the First Peoples Principles of Learning (developed in 2008) was very positive.[3]

In 2016 at a meeting of network leaders, the team decided to combine the networks into one—now known as the Networks of Inquiry and Indigenous Education (NOIIE). We have made considerable progress on our equity and quality goals in the past few decades—and we still have a long way to go before every learner, regardless of their gender, race, orientation, or background, crosses the stage with dignity, purpose, and options. Perseverance, commitment, and courageous leadership are all required for us to reach 100%.

From our own experiences, especially as female leaders, we know that leadership can sometimes be lonely. We know how important it is to create appreciative spaces, where vulnerability is seen as a sign of strength and not a weakness, where courage and fear aren't mutually exclusive, and where it is acceptable to be deeply curious. For many educators, the network has become a space where everyone can leave their formal role at the door, enter as a learner, and focus on the work that needs to be done.

TRANSFORMATION REQUIRED

We have all heard that education systems designed in the last century must change to meet the needs of our learners and our societies today. We know that schools must be transformed to engage young people. Accepting these views is relatively easy. The trickier questions involve knowing what this transformation will look like and how we can achieve it.

We have been interested in understanding school leadership and in developing new leaders for a considerable period of time. Working with hundreds of educators in graduate programs in British Columbia at three different universities over the past two decades has given us a broad perspective. In 2009, we wrote *Leadership Mindsets: Innovation and Learning in the Transformation of Schools* to explore some of the key areas of leadership that we had observed in our strongest school and network leaders. A clear sense of purpose and inquiry competencies were important features of this book, and their importance is just as significant today.

In their provocative book, *Leapfrogging Inequality: Remaking Education to Help Young People Thrive*, Rebecca Winthrop and her colleagues from the Brookings Institution in Washington, DC, argue that inequality is far too prevalent locally and globally. These scholars urge us to link successful innovations in networks to speed up the range of more equitable outcomes in developing systems by leaping over obstacles or barriers pervasive in more developed jurisdictions. They note:

> In many areas of the world the leapfrog mindset is alive and well. Children from poor and wealthy families alike are participating in new approaches that have shown impressive results in changing how schooling is delivered, what is taught, and how teaching is done. This richness of education innovations holds promise for leapfrogging—addressing skills inequality and skills uncertainty—especially if the education innovations community can do a better job of mitigating current gaps and governments can provide a conducive environment for effective innovations to thrive and be scaled up.[4]

Leapfrogging Inequality argues for the development of learning systems that place curiosity at the centre of the learning and teaching process and settings in which hands-on, playful, and experiential learning are centre stage. We agree with this system-changing challenge. We see the leadership teams involved in Spirals work making a big contribution to this dramatic shift—in individual schools and in networks—across a wide range of jurisdictions.

SCHOOL COMMUNITIES THAT ARE CHANGING EXPERIENCES FOR THEIR LEARNERS

We have learned a great deal from the educators in BC and increasingly from around the world who have entered into the networked space of inquiry and connections. Those school communities that are making the most difference for their learners share five important foundational qualities:

They are clear on their purpose. They know what they are doing and why they are doing it.

They are persistently curious. They ask questions, they listen to their learners, and they listen to each other.

They demonstrate a growth mindset. They believe that with effort, support, and strategies they can and will improve.

They are committed to equity. They deliberately identify barriers that predict success or failure, and they intentionally disrupt them. They take an active stance to eliminate racism.

Finally, **they work as teams** both within their schools and across their communities.

The global pandemic uprooted many of the traditional givens for school systems. Ideas about place and space, assessments, lesson plans, grading systems, and the concept of classroom shifted on an almost daily basis. While some educational communities expressed a longing for a return to "normal," many others seized the opportunity to make creative changes based on the needs of learners. The purpose of this book is to provide inquiry teams with an approach to dramatically changing the experiences of young people based on evidence about what makes a difference to learners and to their learning—evidence that is being applied in real schools in real communities doing the hard work of transformation.

Although reformers like to argue the relative merits of improvement, innovation, and accountability, these distinctions are not as relevant to practitioners who may be struggling to make learning more engaging at this moment in their particular context. Through a disciplined approach to collaborative inquiry, resulting in new learning and new actions, educators, learners, their families, and involved community members are gaining the confidence, the insights, and the mindsets required to design powerful new approaches to learning. This process is transforming their schools and their districts. Innovative learning environments are being created and sustained.

We believe that innovation floats on a sea of inquiry. We also believe that curiosity is a driver for change. Creating the conditions in schools and learning settings where curiosity is encouraged, developed, and sustained is essential to opening up thinking, changing practice, and creating dramatically more innovative approaches to learning and teaching. As educators, we all want to engage with ideas and practices that make the biggest possible difference.

THE SPIRAL OF INQUIRY AND INDIGENOUS WAYS OF KNOWING

In our early days with NOIIE, we asked schools to engage in a year-long cycle of inquiry and then to publicly share what differences they had made. When we discovered the research of Helen Timperley, a professor of education at the University of Auckland, we knew that we needed to combine our case study research from BC with her research on high-impact teacher professional learning. Lorna Earl, an assessment expert from the University of Toronto, brought us together for a think tank in Northern Colorado during mud season. Cooped up over three cold and damp days, we generated an exhaustive list of ideas we thought were essential for contemporary school leaders. We called this list the "theory of everything" or, more informally, the TOE job. We decided we had to narrow the focus just a bit and agreed to meet with our new friend from New Zealand in various parts of the world to see where our ideas converged.

Together we experienced an Antarctic front sweeping across Waiheke Island in New Zealand and a mould-infested condo in Honolulu. We debated every idea and every word, and we became good friends. The Spiral of Inquiry process is the result of this collaboration.

A number of publications emerged from our time together. In 2013, the two of us wrote *Spirals of Inquiry: For Equity and Quality* as a publication for principals and vice-principals in BC. In 2014, we published a monograph with Helen Timperley entitled *A Framework for Transforming Learning in Schools: Innovation and the Spiral of Inquiry*. In 2017, we were asked by C21 Canada to write a playbook version of our original *Spirals of Inquiry*, and this has since been translated into Swedish, Spanish, Catalan, and Welsh. This book builds on what we have learned over the past decade as inquiry teams apply the Spiral of Inquiry in a variety of settings. It expands on the original key ideas, provides current research evidence connected to the stages of the Spiral, and uses examples from schools in a range of jurisdictions to illustrate the ways in which leadership teams are applying these ideas.

The image of the spiral was chosen deliberately. Many action research cycles are illustrated as a circle with a beginning and an end. The spiral reflects a never-ending process of curiosity, growth, learning, acting, and reflecting. The spiral shape holds a special significance in a range of Indigenous cultures. For many Indigenous peoples in North America, the spiral represents the evolution and growth of the spirit, the "broadening of consciousness."[5] It is a symbol of change and development.

The First Peoples Principles of Learning represent a starting point for identifying common elements in learning and teaching that exist in First Nations' societies in BC. One of the nine principles is that "Learning is holistic, reflexive, reflective, experiential, and relational." A further principle is that "learning requires patience and time."[6]

While we accept the need for patience, we also need purposeful action for things to change. Bringing to life the calls to action from the Truth and Reconciliation Commission (TRC) in Canada has started and is very much a work in progress.[7] The discovery in June 2021 of the unmarked graves of 215 children who died at the Kamloops Residential School on the territory of the Tk'emlúps te Secwépemc First Nation rocked the consciousness of Canadians and emphasized, yet again, the importance of education as a path to reconciliation.

Leona Prince is the District Principal of Aboriginal Education in the Nechako Lakes School District in British Columbia. She is a member of the Lake Babine Nation and comes from Nak'azdli Whut'en. She also belongs to the Lakh Tsa Mis Yu (Beaver) Clan. In March 2021, Leona spoke at an international conference (International Congress for School Effectiveness and Improvement [ICSEI]) as part of a team from the Networks of Inquiry and Indigenous Education. Here are her observations about the connection between the Spiral of Inquiry and the work of reconciliation:

Throughout my career as an educator I have always gravitated towards tools that recognize and affirm the rich diversity that we have here in BC. After becoming involved with NOIIE, I came to the realization that this framework is a tool for reconciliation. This is not something that I say lightly. I firmly believe that Indigenous pedagogy is fluid, based in relationships, and has multiple entry points where all can engage in learning. These are all things that are true of this model of learning, as well. Most importantly, the Spiral of Inquiry places our children at the center of all knowing, being, and doing. This is an iterative model that is process-driven, which mirrors Indigenous culture and knowledge practices. There is no expected end, but an infinite opportunity to improve on our skills and collective knowledge. This is what current-day public education should look like and what we aspire to achieve. We should value, as a system, process over a product-driven pedagogy. There is a danger to being product-driven, because there is a finality to it, and it limits the potential of our children and by extension our future within this province and country.

The foundation of the inquiry process is relationships. This reminds me of the original relationships of this country and the intention moving forward. The original relationships between Indigenous and Settler nations were built on the idea of mutual respect and mutual understanding, two canoes moving together along the same path. These agreements were to last "as long as the grass grows, the river flows and the sun rises in the east and sets in the west," in perpetuity, like the spiral. Throughout our history we have forgotten those intentions, and tools like the Spirals of Inquiry can help us remember and re-establish that knowledge and process those truths. Inquiry is the Truth in TRC. It helps us affirm the foundations that we are starting from and gives us an opportunity to be honest about the work that we need to do, together. There is no other process that has validated Indigenous Knowledges and has promoted growth more than this model in BC. *Mesiy.*[8]

As Leona so thoughtfully points out, the Spiral of Inquiry invites you into a new, respectful, professional learning space. It asks you to engage in a process that will include surprises and cause you to sometimes feel uncomfortable. It can also be deeply satisfying as you make tangible progress in addressing real learner-related challenges. It is difficult to work out more effective ways to do things before you have a clear understanding of what is currently happening and why. The Spiral asks you initially to suspend judgment on how to "fix" things that are not going well. You need to talk with—and listen to—the learners themselves right from the start. You need to exercise patience and to take your time. The Spiral challenges often long-held biases and assumptions, and requires you to engage in professional learning with an activist stance.

This book reflects our desire to honour the work underway in network schools, to build on the experiences and wisdom of inquiry leaders across countries, to provoke new thinking, and to provide some specific strategies for school teams ready to get started—or keen to go deeper—in leapfrogging inequality and creating genuine equity. The stories included in this book reflect the work in schools we have visited and the educators for whom we have the greatest respect and affection. Although the names of the people and of the schools have been changed, the stories and the spirit of their work are very real.

This book is designed to help teams get started or to go deeper with the Spiral of Inquiry. The first chapter outlines some of the foundational ideas and the research behind the Spiral. Chapters 2 through 4 provide a more in-depth dive into the first three stages of the Spiral—Scanning, Focusing, and Developing a Hunch. We chose to divide the new learning stage into two chapters, so chapter 5 introduces areas for new learning that many network schools are finding especially helpful while chapter 6 provides a series of considerations for inquiry leadership teams as they design New Professional Learning for their colleagues. Chapters 7 and 8 complete the final two stages of the Spiral—Taking Action and Checking. Chapter 9 provides some examples of the ways in which networks across a range of jurisdictions are working together to build equity and quality for all learners.

Each chapter concludes with a brief summary of the key points that we think are most important for you to consider. You will also find a series of questions designed to prompt learning conversations with your team or to serve as prompts for book club meetings. Finally, because this book is all about leadership for change, we will suggest a few specific moves for formal leaders to consider each step along the way.

Let's get started.

1

PURPOSE, CURIOSITY, AND MINDSET

Three Foundational Ideas

What motivates you as an educator?
What do you wonder about?

In her early 20s, Linda found herself teaching in a North London primary school. There she met Ronald, a little boy with endless vitality who slept in a chest of drawers, as there was not enough room in the single bed for him and all his siblings. Judy spent two of her formative years as a teacher in a remote community where jobs were scarce and the future for all but the very fortunate was uncertain. The despair she felt hearing that three boys in her class engaged in a suicide pact the year after she moved out of town has haunted her. Judy never stopped wondering what could have stopped this tragedy. Linda has never stopped wondering what happened to Ronald. These experiences, along with many others, have fuelled in us a passion for social justice and the drive to make schools a place where hope is nurtured, options are expanded, and futures are created.

AS EDUCATORS,[1] YOU have undoubtedly all had moments of outrage when you struggled with unfairness, injustice, poverty, and inequity. The Spiral framework has its roots in moral purpose. The process involves deep listening and challenges often long-held biases and assumptions. It requires inquiry teams to engage in professional curiosity with a growth-oriented mindset.

In this chapter, we will provide you with a rationale for three foundational ideas and a brief description of the stages of the Spiral itself. In the following chapters, we will dive more deeply into each of the stages, always coming back to the central purposes of equity and quality.

WHY CLARITY OF PURPOSE MATTERS

In leadership teams, it's important for you to be clear on your shared purpose as you re-design the learning experiences of the young people you serve. When our commitment is to equity and quality, simply providing the opportunity for learning is not enough. Comments such as "I've done my best to teach them; it's not my problem if they didn't learn" are completely unacceptable. As educators, it is not only our problem, it is our professional responsibility to lift every learner. The days of it being acceptable for some young people to leave school with marginal skills and minimal knowledge, lacking the capacity to participate fully in society, are long behind us.

We like how the Australian state of New South Wales conveys a purposeful feeling in their motto: "Every learner is known, valued and cared for." Building cultures where this motto comes to life is not an easy task. We need schools to be centres of learning and connection for everyone.

Historically, schools have served a sorting purpose, determining which students will go on to university, which students will access some post-secondary training, and which students will go directly to work. In our complex, uncertain, interconnected, and volatile world, we need much more from our schools. One way of illustrating this is to show the shifts required if we are to move more quickly from sorting to learning systems.

FROM SORTING	TO	LEARNING
A focus on instruction and academic achievement		A focus on deeper forms of learning and well-being
Summative assessment for grading and reporting		Formative assessment for coaching and learner agency
Teaching in isolation		Teaching teams working as learning communities
Competition between schools		Networking and collaboration across schools and with communities
Leadership by role/focus on the individual		Leadership by contribution/focus on the team
Externalized accountability		Local internalized commitment and responsibility and capacity-building
Maintaining the status quo		Passionately pursuing equity and quality for all learners

Tackling the challenge of creating higher quality and more equitable learning systems for all young people is tough, complex work. It is not work for the faint of heart, nor can it rely on the lone heroic educator. Changing systems requires teamwork, courage, commitment, collaboration, curiosity, and an intense sense of moral purpose.

Right now, we encourage you to think about why you are interested in engaging in Spirals of Inquiry.

- What drives you to want to change the experiences of your learners?
- Do you have in mind a group of learners whose challenges trouble you? Who is the Ronald that you wonder about?
- Can you articulate clearly the purpose for your school?
- Is this purpose broadly understood and shared by your school community?
- To what extent do your day-to-day actions match your values?
- Are you ready to have your assumptions challenged?
- Are you curious about what is really going on for your learners? Are you ready to listen to them?

STARTING WITH MORAL PURPOSE

Simon Sinek, in his widely viewed Ted Talk[2] and then in his book *Start With Why,* uses the image of a golden circle to explain why productive leadership always starts with purpose.

He claims that virtually everyone in an organization or school can say *what* they do. For instance, "I teach history." He further claims that most people can say *how* they do this: "I deliver curriculum, I assess progress, I provide feedback, and I report to parents." He argues, however, that considerably fewer people in many organizations can give a clear answer to the question of *why* they do what they do. The main message here is that some leaders start and finish their thinking at the outermost circle. They ask themselves what they are doing and seldom think any further.

The Golden Circle

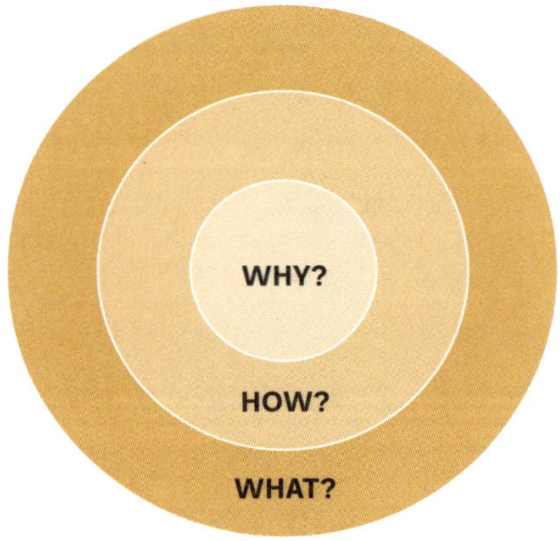

Leaders operating at the outer edge of the circle can lose sight of their actual goal and, as a result, fail at their main task of challenging and encouraging people to the greatest possible extent in their development, in their thinking, and in their actions. We have witnessed some educators in leadership roles who do the job and run their schools irrespective of the impact of their actions on their staff or their students.

We have also seen many leadership teams that are highly motivated by the conviction that they can help contribute to a more just world through high-quality education for everyone. As truly effective school leaders, their concern is not just about *what* to do. They know that *why* and *how* they do what they are doing matters.

In our work with hundreds of schools in a range of countries, we have seen firsthand the importance of clarity of purpose *before* embarking on a new initiative or embracing a new program. When we know *why* we are making a change—whether it is designing deeper forms of learning, creating more inclusive and equitable learning settings, or prioritizing environmental sustainability—the chances of persevering when things inevitably get tough are much better.

The educators we work with are much more motivated by challenging, hard goals than by incremental goals such as those focused exclusively on raising achievement scores a few percentage points. The idea of "HARD Goals" comes from the work of Mark Murphy. His research finds that "HARD Goals," which "are Heartfelt, Animated, Required, and Difficult," can "light up the brain and encourage great performance."[3]

This happens when we:

- genuinely believe in the importance of the goal (it is Heartfelt)
- bring it to life through our work every day (it is Animated)
- are driven by a sense of social justice and urgency for equity (it is Required)
- understand that achieving it will be truly challenging (it is Difficult)

In *The Infinite Game*, Simon Sinek talks about a just cause as the truly big idea or ideal vision of what we want to create. This is a cause that we stand for and believe in. Broadly speaking, the Spiral of Inquiry is rooted in a vision of equity and quality for all learners in every context, regardless of their starting point. This is our just cause, and it has developed over time into three big goals:

1. **Every learner crosses the stage with dignity, purpose, and options**
   For us, crossing the stage is a metaphor for young people moving from adolescence to adulthood. Dignity implies that learners have the freedom to express their authentic selves without fear of being judged, that they feel safe both physically and psychologically, and that they are recognized for their strengths and contributions. A sense of purpose and genuine options for the future help equip young people with the confidence to make their way in a complex world.

2. **Every learner leaves our settings more curious than when they arrived**
   Too often we have seen, to our dismay, the natural curiosity that young children bring to their early learning diminish in some school settings. The big questions about how the world works are reduced to "What is on the test?" or "What are we doing today?" Similarly, we see new teachers entering the profession eager to make a difference. It is tragic to see this enthusiasm diminished over time by static or negative cultures. We now know a great deal about how to develop inquiry-mindedness for educators and for students. It is our goal that every teacher becomes more curious about their practice and about their impact on learners. The Spiral is designed to open up space for adult curiosity and to create more curiosity-infused environments for learners of all ages.

3. **Every learner gains an understanding of and respect for Indigenous ways of knowing and develops an anti-racist stance**
   The experience of colonization in many countries, including our own, has had lasting negative consequences for First Peoples. Understanding our various histories and the impact of colonization is a first step toward reconciliation and to creating more socially just societies. The Black Lives Matter movement is raising awareness of the insidious effects of racism within many cultures. Understanding and respecting Indigenous ways of knowing will help us in the hard work of reconciliation.

We share these with you as examples of the kinds of goals that have evolved from two decades of challenging conversations within and across inquiry-oriented schools. We offer them simply as a starting point for your own conversations about what the big purpose is for you, your school, and your network. And we encourage you to think about how, through engaging in Spirals of Inquiry, you can get closer to achieving your own bold goals.

WHY CURIOSITY IS SO IMPORTANT

A careful look at learning systems around the world leads us to believe that those systems with teachers and formal leaders who use their collective curiosity in learning teams are the ones that are doing the strongest job of helping their learners with the deeper forms of learning that are required today. John Watkins, Amelia Peterson, and Jal Mehta argue:

> All over the world, school is changing. Faced with all the possibilities, inequities, anxieties, and complexities of contemporary life, educators and students alike are balking at an inherited approach to schooling that does little to prepare students for those challenges. They are finding ways to orient student work around meaningful questions and practices, replacing coverage with mastery of knowledge, busy-work with disciplined creativity, and one-size-fits-all with a diversity of promising approaches. Some of them have described this as a reorientation towards **deeper learning.**[4]

Jal Mehta and Sarah Fine have also introduced the notion of symmetry in educational change.[5] Educators in many systems want young people to be curious, inquiry-minded thinkers, thoughtful problem-solvers, and wise decision-makers. The idea of symmetry is straightforward—if we want these outcomes for our students, then we need to strengthen adult competencies in these same areas. For young people to be curious, they need to be supported and surrounded by adults who are equally curious themselves. We need to place inquiry-based approaches at the centre of our own collective professional learning. This requires a shift in focus toward developing collaborative capacity among educators.

Curiosity is crucial in this evolving paradigm. Bryan Goodwin describes informational curiosity as the need to "find more information on a particular topic. It drives us to delve deeply into something and get smarter about it. It's often associated with an inner drive to learn, stick-to-itiveness and a relentless pursuit of knowledge just beyond our reach."[6]

In thinking about how this inner drive develops, we are fortunate to be able to draw on the work of Susan Engel. She has researched and written about the development of curiosity in childhood. Her book *The Hungry Mind* reports on a study she conducted with colleagues in elementary classrooms. They were looking for the specific teacher behaviours that encouraged active investigation driven by the personal or shared curiosity of the students.

The researchers were exploring one big question: "What is it in a classroom that serves to encourage or discourage investigation?" They discovered something surprisingly simple: "We found there was a direct link between how much the teacher smiled and talked in an encouraging manner and the level of curiosity the children in the room expressed."[7] The research team also found that teachers who encouraged curiosity took an invitational stance to learning. They noted that this kind of teacher asks questions of students, of colleagues, and of herself.

The curiosity-building teacher also shares her own interests, including the things that captivated her curiosity when she was the same age as her students. "She looks things up in books or on the internet. She looks out the window with interest, and she watches as students make things and play with each other. Her expression of curiosity provides an adult model of inviting curiosity in others."[8] *The Hungry Mind* concludes "that one of the things children learn from adults is what kind of intellectual stance to take—contemplative or not, interested or not, detached or not."[9]

Most principals, as they understand more about the crucial role of curiosity in learning, appreciate the various ways in which their teachers individually spark and sustain learner curiosity. Developing and sustaining curiosity cannot, however, be the sole responsibility of a single classroom teacher. It needs to become a school-wide commitment such as is evidenced in the commitment to curiosity in the schools in the Expeditionary Learning Network.[10] Compassionate curiosity is a practice developed from trauma-informed teaching that asks teachers to act as non-judgmental investigators so they can better understand their students.

Principals can build a culture of curiosity by modelling their own curiosity about what is going on for their learners as well as by being open about the big questions they are exploring themselves. A simple opening strategy like providing the opportunity for teachers to engage in conversations about why they became teachers in the first place links the concept of purpose with respectful and compassionate curiosity.

WHY GROWTH MINDSET MATTERS

Carol Dweck, a leading researcher in the area of developmental psychology, describes mindset change in this way:

> Mindset change is not about picking up a few pointers here and there. It's about seeing things in a new way. When people—couples, coaches and athletes, managers and workers, parents and children, teachers and students—change to a growth mindset, they change from a **judge-and-be-judged** framework to a **learn-and-help-learn** framework. Their commitment is to growth and growth takes plenty of time, effort, and mutual support.[11]

This work of shifting mindsets in a growth direction is neither easy nor trivial work. It is highly consequential work. Jo Boaler, who has expertise in helping young people develop more positive attitudes to learning mathematics, points out in her book *Limitless Mind* that "the result of fixed brain thinking is that we have a nation (and world) filled with underachieving people who have been limited by ideas that could and should be changed."[12]

Limitless Mind describes six keys to learning from a growth perspective:

1. Every time we learn, our brains form, strengthen, or connect neural pathways. We need to replace the idea that learning ability is fixed, with the recognition that we are all on a growth journey.[13]
2. The times when we are struggling and making mistakes are the best times for brain growth.[14]
3. When we change our beliefs, our bodies and our brains physically change as well.[15]

4. Neural pathways and learning are optimized when considering ideas with a multidimensional approach.[16]

5. Speed of thinking is not a measure of aptitude. Learning is optimized when we approach ideas and life with creativity and flexibility.[17]

6. Connecting with people and ideas enhances neural pathways and learning.[18]

As you engage with the Spiral of Inquiry, we encourage you to stay open to the possibility that the struggles you will inevitably have will change your perceptions and your beliefs. This is all part of the process. As Debbie Leighton Stephens, a wise Indigenous network leader, has taught us: "If you aren't squirming, you aren't learning."

A powerful example of how a focus on growth mindset can help to interrupt the colonization in a school serving Native American learners comes from the work of Stephanie Fryberg, Rebecca Covarrubias, and Jacob A. Burack. This research team working with the Tulalip Tribes in Northwestern Washington introduced the predominantly non-Indigenous staff members at two local elementary schools to the growth mindset literature. Initially they were asked to focus on their own core cultural beliefs about potential, but eventually the links were made to negative ability stereotypes and low expectations for racial-ethnic minority and low-income students. These researchers state:

> The colonizing power of these stereotypes is that they de-legitimatize Indigenous ways of being—they reinforce the belief that Indigenous students need to change or are un-fixable—and ultimately require Indigenous students to "be Indigenous" *in relation to* European Americans.[19]

The team used the mindset literature to reconceptualize ideas about who has the potential to grow and change with hard work and skill development. They concluded that reconceptualizing ideas about potential had the unanticipated benefit of helping teachers be more open-minded and less defensive with respect to learning about culture and race issues. Teachers became less afraid to ask questions about Native American students and their families, and the climate of race- and culture-focused training changed. The focus on growth mindset coupled with expanding teachers' cultural toolkits over the three-year period of the study led to dramatic improvements in academic outcomes.

We have had the good fortune of spending time in leading-edge schools where growth mindset has become a way of life. Regardless of the country or the context, a defining characteristic of these schools is that they have strong learning cultures that support the development of growth mindsets. We can sense right away when a school has a spirit of "We are all here to learn, and we can help each other get stronger." In these schools, learners are not paralyzed by the fear of making mistakes. They understand that making mistakes is a healthy part of improving. Teachers are not afraid to ask questions about race and culture. They are open to new learning, and they are willing to challenge their own biases and assumptions.

As you begin your journey into the Spiral, we encourage you to accept that this is challenging work and you will make mistakes. The only way you can really go wrong is through not being open to learning from your mistakes—or, even worse, not trying at all. Clarity of purpose, a spirit of curiosity, and a growth mindset are foundational to the Spiral of Inquiry. Let's take a quick look next at the Spiral itself, knowing that in the following chapters we will explore each stage in greater depth.

THE SPIRAL OF INQUIRY

There are several features that distinguish the Spiral of Inquiry from other action research approaches. The Spiral starts with understanding what is going on for learners and requires intentional listening to them. The Spiral:

- is designed for teams and requires collaboration.
- is specifically designed to change outcomes for learners in areas that really matter.
- requires a deep understanding of learning and appreciation for the experiences of learners.
- uses terminology that respects teachers' judgment, their lived experiences, and their appreciation of clear language.
- when used intentionally and thoroughly, helps develop a culture of participatory democracy across the school.

The Spiral of Inquiry involves six key stages: Scanning, Focusing, Developing a Hunch, engaging in New Professional Learning, Taking Action, and Checking that a big enough difference has been made, then re-engaging to consider what is next.

Although the stages of the Spiral overlap, paying attention to each stage is critical in achieving the greatest benefit for all learners. At every phase, inquiry teams ask themselves three important questions: "What's going on for our learners?" "How do we know?" "Why does this matter?"

The first two questions prompt inquiry teams to check constantly that learners are at the heart of what they do, and that all decisions are based on thoughtful evidence from direct observations in addition to formal evidence sources. The third question helps to ground teams in the importance of the direction they are pursuing.

Scanning
What's going on for our learners?

Just about everyone in a school community has opinions about what is going on for learners. Scanning is all about collecting a variety of rich evidence about what is really taking place. *This means we must listen to learners and be open to what they have to say.*

In a reasonable amount of time (usually three to four weeks), inquiry leadership teams gather and consider useful information in key areas of learning. Understanding the degree to which students feel emotionally connected to adults in their learning environment and the degree to which they fully understand the key learning goals are critically important in scanning.[20] An initial scan draws on the transversal learning principles from a western perspective identified by David Istance and Hanna Dumont.[21] A thorough scan incorporates a First Peoples' perspective to determine the extent to which learners' experiences are reflective of what is known and valued about learning.

Focusing
Where are we going to place our attention?

In the Focusing stage, inquiry leadership teams ask themselves: "Where are we going to concentrate our professional energies so that we can change the experiences and results for our learners?" Sometimes, the scanning process reveals a puzzling picture—one that requires deeper investigation. For example, an initial scan may identify that some learners are deeply engaged in their learning while others are not. Some learners are making good progress in developing key competencies; others are stalled. Some learners feel well supported by the adults in their school; others do not.

At the heart of the Focusing stage is gaining greater clarity about the situation for learners by hearing from them directly before deciding on a course of action. Unlike the scanning process, which requires a broad perspective, the Focusing stage requires choosing amongst competing priorities. Having a process for deciding the major area of focus is where a practical decision-making framework can be invaluable. You will be introduced to this framework in chapter 3.

Developing a Hunch
What's leading to this situation and how are we contributing to it?

The Hunch stage asks the inquiry team to probe for evidence that will clarify what is leading to the present situation and, most important, how we—the professionals—are contributing to that situation. Everyone generally has hunches about why things are the way they are. Sometimes these views are passionately held. Getting them on the table in such a way that they can be discussed and tested is fundamental to moving forward as a team. For example, school teams involved in anti-racism work will use the Hunch stage to explore how their biases and assumptions may be limiting some options for their learners. Developing confidence and skill in having challenging conversations is part of the Hunch stage.

New Professional Learning
Where and how will we learn more about what to do?

All phases of the Spiral involve learning, but at this stage educators engage with the specific task of carefully determining and designing new professional learning. To do so, inquiry leadership teams ask themselves, "How and where can we learn more about what to do?"

The content for new professional learning will emerge from testing out the hunches about what is leading to the situation for learners. External expertise may be required depending on the context of the school and the capacity of the staff in the area of focus. A key responsibility for the leadership team will be to encourage the development of adaptive expertise for all staff members.

Taking Action
What will we do differently?

This is the stage in the Spiral of Inquiry where new learning leads to new practices. Once teams have acquired new knowledge about the practices that will help learners, it is time to take action by jumping across what Jeffrey Pfeffer and Robert Sutton call the knowing-doing gap. At this stage, the inquiry team needs to ensure that all those involved are encouraged and supported to try out the new practices.

Teams must make sure that there is plenty of opportunity for dialogue, observation, and reflection. Sometimes second, third, and fourth tries are required without fear of judgment or failure. Changing practice can feel risky for many teachers, and inquiry teams will need to find ways to make the risk-taking less risky.

Checking
Have we made *enough* of a difference?

The purpose of the Spiral of Inquiry is to make a difference for learners in areas of real importance. It can't be assumed that changes in practice or the introduction of innovative approaches always lead to substantive changes. It is in this part of the Spiral that inquiry teams ask whether they are making enough of a difference for enough of their learners. Creating an agreement ahead of time about what evidence to look for as well as what will constitute enough of a difference will be key. The Spiral doesn't end with checking—it takes teams to a new place of scanning in which the Spiral goes deeper and wider.

The Spiral of Inquiry builds on what strong teams of highly effective educators often do intuitively. By making these practices explicit and by providing real school examples, we hope to stimulate your curiosity. We encourage you to get started—or to dive in more deeply.

BIG IDEAS FROM CHAPTER 1

- Get clear on your purpose for engaging in Spirals work. Making significant changes to the experiences of your learners is difficult, and you need to have your own HARD goals clearly in your mind as you get started.
- Understand how important it is to stay curious. Acknowledge that there is a lot that you don't know. Be ready to have your assumptions challenged, and acknowledge that uncertainty is part of learning.
- Recognize that the Spiral is specifically designed to change outcomes for learners in areas that really matter and requires a deep understanding of what is going on for learners.
- Approach this work with a growth mindset—the belief that we are all here to learn, and we can help each other get stronger.

QUESTIONS FOR LEARNING CONVERSATIONS

1. When you consider the need to transform systems for equity and quality, what are some of the current strengths of your school that reflect a learning orientation as opposed to a sorting function?
2. What is your "just cause" as an educator? What gets you up in the morning and eager to get to work?
3. What are the current goals in your school or system? Would you characterize them as "hard" goals? Why or why not?
4. How is risk-taking encouraged in your school? How are you developing a growth mindset for learners of all ages?
5. The idea of symmetry is straightforward. For example, if we want our young people to be curious and inquiry-minded, then we need to develop adult competencies in these areas. How might the idea of symmetry change the ways in which school teams design professional learning?

LEADERSHIP MOVES

- Recruit a diverse team (ideally four to seven members) as a start. Don't limit your team exclusively to teachers. Depending on your context, support staff, cultural support workers, educational assistants, students, and community members can play an important role.
- Build in time during the day for the team to meet. Create a regular (e.g., every two to three weeks) meeting schedule that works for the group. Think about the best location for the team to meet and what refreshments will indicate that their contributions are valued.
- Be present, avoid any interruptions, and make space for others to lead.

2

SCANNING

The Starting Point for Team Inquiry

What's going on for our learners?
How do we know? Why does it matter?

"These kids are just …." "What we need are …." "Why don't we change the timetable, the bell schedule, the curriculum …." "If only they would, then we could …." How many of these conversations have you overheard at staff meetings or planning sessions? How often have you heard about a new technology solution that is "guaranteed" to create better results? How often have you seen an apparently promising new idea be consigned to the junk heap of failed initiatives after a few years? Have you ever heard "We tried that before and it didn't work"?

THE SPIRAL OF Inquiry is a framework based on what great teams of educators do naturally. It is not a program. It is a professional way of being that can lead to dramatically different experiences for learners.

All too often it is adults who decide what is right or wrong with learners—and what is good for them—without involving students themselves in either identifying issues or developing solutions. Deciding what is going on for learners without their input lacks respect and is less likely to lead to productive change. One of the key features of the Spiral is the direct involvement of learners from the beginning and throughout the whole process.

This kind of work requires a team. It is too difficult for an individual leader or teacher, all on their own, to make substantive changes that result in greater equity for learners. It also requires high levels of motivation and energy. And yet, in the real world of schools, not everyone starts as a team player, nor does everyone begin with enthusiasm. We have found that engaging in an inquiry process that addresses genuine learner-related challenges helps build the commitment that is required over the long haul. It is important to get started even if everyone is not on board right at the beginning.

The Scanning stage of the Spiral asks you to be genuinely curious about your learners and to stay open to all kinds of new information and insights. The scanning process starts to create the motivation and energy for further engagement. It also ensures a much richer understanding of student experiences and will help you avoid the traps of your own assumptions, biases, judgments, and perceptions. A thorough scan establishes the foundation for future learning and informed action.

The scan needs to be wide enough so that key areas—like the arts, understanding the natural world, Indigenous perspectives, physical activity, empathy, ethical behaviour, resilience, and social-emotional learning—do not get missed. It is very important to avoid restricting the scanning process only to areas for which evidence is easily available.

Most schools have detailed information about academic learning outcomes, especially in the areas of literacy and numeracy. Many schools collect data about behaviour referrals. The ready availability of such evidence does not mean it gives a full picture of what is going on for and with young people. Teams need to get underneath the data sources to understand what these numbers are actually saying.

Educator observation provides a valuable source of information about learners. Just watching how young people interact on the playground, in an online environment, or in a learning commons setting, and seeing how they respond when learning outside the classroom, approaching a new challenge, or welcoming new students to their class can tell you a lot about their emotional connectedness, their adaptability, and maybe even their resilience. If you are systematic as a team about observing learners in a range of situations, you will gain invaluable information during this part of the process.

Scanning requires you to look at the experiences of the learners in the school as a whole, as well as in individual classrooms or learning settings. This means asking some difficult questions. For instance, "Is it all right for some learners to feel a sense of belonging while others are feeling less connected to the school?" "Is it acceptable for learners in one room to experience challenging and engaging tasks while in another class the learning activities are much less engaging?" "Why does this group of students have such trouble collaborating in the classroom when they work together effectively outside?"

TWO KEY QUESTIONS AS A STARTING POINT

Once educators open themselves up to being curious about what is going on for our learners, the potential areas of interest can be limitless. We have found that by starting with two key questions, teams become more curious about what is going on in a range of areas. When learners experience being listened to with respect, they feel valued and begin to develop a greater sense of agency. As one

Year 6 (i.e., Grade 6) girl said to her teacher, "This is my best day ever. No one has asked me about my learning before."

1. Can you name two adults in this school who believe you will be a success in life?

Kimberley Schonert-Reichl is a leading thinker in the area of social-emotional learning. She and her colleagues have developed a survey with a series of indicators for student social-emotional well-being that is now used in a number of jurisdictions.[1] There are forty items on the survey that provide a lot of valuable information. For the purpose of scanning by inquiry teams, however, we encourage teachers to focus on areas with a significant impact and over which they have control. With the advice of the research team, we landed on this first big question and one follow-up:

> "*Can you name two adults in this school who believe you will be a success in life?*" And then (if you get a positive response), you ask, "*How do they show you?*"

There are a number of critical points about this question. First, the evidence on resiliency indicates that a positive adult can keep a young person on track.[2] For all our learners, and especially for those who are most vulnerable, we need to make sure that there are at least two adults in the school who know, value, and encourage them.

Prior to asking this question, there needs to be some dialogue about the meaning of success in life. Teachers have found personal stories, literature, short video clips, and student experiences helpful in developing a wider picture of what success means. Individual definitions of success may vary, but many define it as being fulfilled, happy, safe, loved, contributing in some way to the greater good, and living a meaningful life. Some teachers adapt this question to ask, "Who in this school has your back, knows you, and believes in you?" The intent of this question is the same. The challenge for inquiry teams is to ask themselves, "Do we know the individual goals and dreams of each of our learners?"

What happens if the learner can't name anyone? Time to take immediate action! A sense of connectedness is so important that you don't need to complete a whole Spiral before moving to action. One of the most effective strategies is called the 2 x 10.[3] If you discover a learner who does not think there is anyone in the school who believes in them, then you commit to connecting with that student individually for two minutes a day, ten days in a row about something personal to them (and nothing to do with school). Find out more about who they are, what they enjoy doing, and what they see themselves doing in the future. In most cases, this is enough to develop a connection and to increase their sense of belonging.

The second part of this question is to name the specific behaviours of the adult who communicates their belief in the learner. The responses to this question initially can be surprising. But from our experience in many different schools, some common themes have emerged. One is the importance of specific, direct communication with individual learners. Another is the positive impact of high expectations and teacher determination in pushing for quality.

Be curious about what your learners have to say—you may be surprised, too. Finally, when you listen to a learner talk about the adults who are making a difference to their sense of self, please don't keep this information to yourself. Sometimes the educators who are best at communicating their belief to a range of young people may not know that this is one of their strengths.

There are many ways in which these questions—and the student responses—can be used to build teacher curiosity. We appreciated the positive responses of teachers at one elementary school where the professional learning meetings always started with short video clips of students talking about the adults in the school who believed in them. This was a great way to create a positive tone right from the start.

Recently, we were interviewing students in a rural high school, and one teacher's name came up repeatedly. One of the common threads was the students' appreciation that when they didn't understand a concept the first time, the teacher would continually look for new ways to explain it until they got it. When we found the teacher and told him what his students had said, he was moved and commented, "I have been teaching twenty years and no one has told me that before." This opened up a conversation that led to this teacher becoming a resource for other teachers—a new teacher-leader in the making.

Be sure to use the positive comments that you hear to build teacher efficacy. And be sure to use the information about those students who are disconnected to move to immediate action. The goal should be 100% of young people able to identify at least two educators who they *know* believe in them.

2. What are you learning and why is it important?

Consciously strengthening social and emotional connections with each learner is a vital part of a powerful inquiry repertoire. It is also critical to ensure that each learner understands the purpose of his or her learning. There is a big difference between learners knowing *what* they are supposed to be doing and learners knowing *why* what they are learning is important. Just posing this second question shifts the focus from simply completing a task toward more purposeful learning.

Learners are only able to answer this question when they have been helped to find personal meaning in the content or topic. Without a clear sense of purpose, many learners become disengaged and lose their sense of curiosity, even as they continue to jump through the hoops of the school system. For learning to be relevant and purposeful, young people need to be in an environment where clarity about the big learning intentions, the big ideas, the big learning goals, or the big questions is clearly evident.

John Hattie and Helen Timperley have written about the importance of feedback from learners to their teachers. They emphasize the necessity of regularly finding out from learners the answers to the following questions:

- Where are you going with your learning?
- How are you going with your learning?
- What is your next step?[4]

Years of experience with inviting educators to explore these questions have taught us to emphasize starting scanning with just this first two-part question: "What are you learning and why is it important?" If you don't get strong answers to this question, there isn't much point in continuing to the next ones.

Our aim is to ensure that *every* learner can articulate what they are learning, why it is important, and how it is connected to their lives. There is a big difference between being able to say *what* they are *doing*—"We are reading about erosion"—and *why* it is important—"We are learning about erosion and how it impacts the sustainability of our island. We want to figure out some strategies for slowing the rate of erosion." As school staff members become more confident with formative assessment strategies and more adept in making connections between the curriculum and the lived experiences of their learners, rich answers like this become the norm.

Asking "What are you learning?" as a general question can be interesting as you find out what really stands out in the mind of the learner. It can also be helpful to ask the question more specifically: "What are you learning about reading non-fiction?" "What are you learning about thinking critically?" "What are you learning about climate change and sustainability?" "What are you learning through your community engagement work?"

During the Scanning stage, knowing how many young people feel a sense of belonging and connectedness to adults in the building and then knowing how many understand what they are learning and why that learning matters are the essential starting points. Equipped with this close-to-the-learner information, leadership teams can make much more informed decisions about productive areas of focus.

THE IMPORTANCE OF LEARNING PRINCIPLES TO SCANNING

In the Scanning stage, we also need to check out the extent to which the experiences of young people in our schools reflect what is currently known about learning. The seven learning principles identified through the Organisation for Economic Co-operation and Development (OECD) study on the nature of learning provide one useful set of lenses.

David Istance and the research team at the Centre for Educational Research and Innovation (CERI) conducted a decade-long study exploring innovative learning environments. The first part of this study involved an international set of papers reflecting current knowledge about the learning sciences. These papers became the foundation for the 2010 OECD publication, *The Nature of Learning*.[5] In the final chapter, David Istance and Hanna Dumont argue that, in order for a learning environment to be truly effective, all seven of the following principles must be evident. A broad scan that includes looking at these seven important learning principles can enrich your inquiry work.

Here are some scanning questions linked to the seven learning principles identified by this research:

1. **The centrality of learners**

   Can learners answer the question "What are you learning?" Can they describe in their own words what they are learning—and why what they are learning is important? Are they able to set specific learning targets and construct their learning through active exploration? Can they use a range of ways to demonstrate their learning?

2. **The social nature of learning**

   Do learners demonstrate the kinds of social and collaborative skills needed for teamwork, citizenship, and the workplace? Are they able to work effectively with different groups of students? Are they able to solve problems peacefully? Do they listen respectfully to each other?

3. **The centrality of emotions to learning**

   Can each learner name at least two adults in the setting who believe he or she will be a success in life? Can they describe how these adults have shown them they believe in them? To what extent are learners able to monitor and manage their own emotions? What strategies do they have to deal with feelings of stress, anger, or anxiety?

4. **Recognizing individual differences**

   Are learners confident that their teachers know their individual strengths, interests, and passions? Do they think their teachers understand what they find difficult or challenging? Do teachers value and use the prior knowledge and cultural backgrounds that learners bring to the setting? Do learners feel respected?

5. **Stretching all students**

   Are learners, regardless of their age, able to teach someone else, and are they able to make a contribution to the community as a whole? Are all learners experiencing demanding, engaging, and challenging work without excessive overload?

6. **Assessment for learning**

   Can learners describe what quality work looks like—and how their work compares to agreed-upon criteria? Do they know their next step? Are learners confident and capable in both giving and receiving feedback with their peers, based on co-constructed criteria?

7. **Building horizontal connections**

Can learners see and understand the connections across content areas? Do they have the opportunity to pursue important questions in depth, or are they restricted to covering the curriculum? To what extent can learners connect with and learn from the broader environment—and from members of their community?

SCANNING INFORMED BY FIRST PEOPLES PRINCIPLES OF LEARNING

In our province of British Columbia (BC), inquiry teams are encouraged to ensure they use the First Peoples Principles of Learning (FPPL) in considering student and adult learning. These principles are a rich source of educational insights from Indigenous cultures that have become embedded in use over thousands of years.

In addition to Métis and Inuit, BC is the home of 203 First Nations whose languages represent seventeen distinct linguistic groups. This diversity means that traditionally there has not been one single expression of education-related principles. There are, however, strong similarities in worldviews and in the ways of knowing and learning among Indigenous peoples in BC. A significant group of Indigenous educators worked together to create the FPPL.[6]

We encourage all inquiry teams to explore these Indigenous principles to see the extent to which the wisdom of Indigenous peoples in BC resonates with your experiences in your contexts, cultures, and traditions. We have found that this holistic view of learning has resonated with educators in every country we have worked with so far.

Here are some scanning questions connected to the FPPL:

- Do learners see what they are learning in school as contributing to their own well-being and to that of their families and communities?
- Are learners developing a deeper sense of place and a stronger connection to the land?
- Do they have a chance to explore and understand the consequences of their actions?
- Do they have the opportunity to learn with and from different age groups and generations?

- To what extent are meaningful, powerful stories part of their experience at school?
- Are they exploring their own identity?
- Are they developing patience?
- Are they learning to care about, respect, and learn from the natural world?

You can see from these sets of questions that the scope for scanning can be very broad. This is why we encourage you to *start* with the two key questions. Once you have a solid understanding of what's going on for your learners in terms of their sense of connectedness and cognitive agency, we expect you will be curious about many other aspects of their learning experiences.

SO, WHAT DOES THIS LOOK LIKE IN PRACTICE?

At this point some short school stories may be helpful.

Middle school

We recently received an email from Robert, a principal of a middle school in the Okanagan Valley in BC. Robert was interested in what Derek, one of his fellow principals, had done to change the culture of his school. He knew that Derek had worked with a small inquiry team to make some significant shifts in a sense of belongingness school-wide. Robert spent some time interviewing Derek and some of his colleagues and then shared with us what he learned.

Derek and his staff had been curious about the degree of engagement and connection, particularly amongst their middle-school boys. They decided to start their Spiral process by asking two clear, straightforward questions:

1. Do you like coming to school?
2. Can you name two or more adults in the school who believe you will be successful in life?

The results of the initial scan were jarring for everyone. It shocked the staff that only 68% of their male students liked coming to school and that only 62% of the boys with Indigenous ancestry could name two adults who believed in their success. As Robert said in his email, "As a statistic the number 38% doesn't seem too bad. But the staff knew the students' faces, their hopes, their struggles, their dreams, and their aspirations. The number sat in the pit of their stomach like undigested food."

After collecting the data, the inquiry team met to brainstorm ways to help students feel more like they wanted to be at school. They talked to the boys, they listened to what they had to say, they did a lot of learning, they moved to informed action and they checked constantly to see if they were making enough of a difference. As Robert said, "The creative force of the team was unleashed to think creatively; they became curious scientists of their own practices."

Over the next two years the staff continued to focus on developing a sense of connectedness. Their concerted actions led to a seismic shift in the experiences of their learners. Robert concluded his email with this statement:

> In the first three months the results collected on a spreadsheet were impressive. However, they are not nearly as impressive as the vibrant joy evident in the faces of students who within a year could confidently answer that they like coming to school and that they have at least two adults at school who believe they will be a success in life.[7]

Secondary school

A few years ago, a suburban secondary school began exploring the learning needs of their students by using the Spiral of Inquiry framework. During a series of learner interviews the inquiry team discovered that homework was a real challenge. Students saw the tasks as lacking meaning and had formed groups to "just get it done." The staff listened to the feedback from their learners. They took a critical look at the quality and quantity of assignments, and they moved to developing more challenging cross-curricular assignments—fewer in number and greater in depth.

Since this initial effort, the staff has engaged in a number of complete cycles through the Spiral. Their confidence has grown, and now they are committed to the tough work of creating a highly inclusive school environment in which every learner is making significant learning gains. They are drawing on the support of a skilled coordinator to infuse the philosophy and practices of the Universal Design for Learning (UDL) into every classroom setting over the next two years.[8]

As the educators became increasingly familiar with the language and the stages of the Spiral, they made their learning visible to their students and their broader community. Student leaders began to become actively involved. At the start, Stewart, the school principal, worked with three senior students who were concerned about the number of younger students who were not involved in any school activities and for whom weekends were especially lonely. After scanning the younger students through a survey and personal interviews, these student leaders created a Friday after-school program. They arranged a wide range of fun and engaging activities. Fifty previously disengaged students got involved in playing games, making friends, and having a great time.

Other senior students watched this initiative and started to be curious about what else was going on for their younger colleagues. The next year another group of student leaders decided to use a Spiral of Inquiry to tackle a troubling issue. They were aware that younger learners were being bullied online, and they raised the issue of cyberbullying with Emily, their vice-principal. Emily explained the Spiral framework, and she encouraged the group to interview younger students about their experiences, to learn as much as they could, and then to design and deliver an intervention program. Over the school year, this inquiry was highly effective in reducing negative online interactions.

At this same school, another group of students expressed their interest in combating racism. Their scanning process is just getting started. Student leadership groups in five other district high schools have heard about these initiatives and have become interested in doing similar work. Researchers from Harvard were approached and are now providing advice to the youth leadership team as they work to deepen their proactive and pro-social inquiry work. The student leaders in this district are becoming a positive force with which to be reckoned.

Elementary school

This story from an elementary school illustrates how scanning can challenge the assumptions of teachers and lead to a deeper focus area. The inquiry at this school began with teachers voicing concerns about the growing levels of anxiety in their intermediate students (Years 4 and 5). Their hunch was that increasing time spent online as well as high parental expectations were the root causes of what they were seeing in class. Their first response was to consider introducing mindfulness training to combat anxiety. Fortunately, before moving to action they realized that the missing piece in their inquiry was that they had yet to listen to the students. They made a commitment to do an in-depth scan.

What emerged after a series of conversations with their young learners was that, while there was some truth to the concerns about technology and parental expectations, a more substantive reason for the increase in anxiety at these particular grade levels was the change in assessment practices in mathematics. The grading practices in math were much more summative in nature than those in language arts and those the students had experienced in their primary program.

This insight led to a change in direction and a much deeper inquiry focused on building teacher confidence in teaching mathematics and strengthening formative assessment practices across the curriculum. Students are now much less anxious and teachers are proud of their learning. The school has become a sought-after hub for professional learning about formative assessment strategies in mathematics.

Middle-school network

Three years ago, a middle school in Northern Australia became curious about the Spiral, and the staff was eager to get started. Deb, their vice-principal, led the team into an inquiry on mathematical understandings. They were off and running, attending workshops, trying out new strategies and in true Australian form, giving new approaches to mathematics a crack. When it came time to share their findings at the network gathering, they decided to ask the key cognitive question of a number of their learners.

They were dismayed by the responses they got to the question "What are you learning in math and why is it important?" Answers like "So I can do well on the test" or "Because I need it for next year" didn't cut it. Deb realized that, in the team's enthusiasm to get started, they forgot to involve their learners in the Scanning stage, and they hadn't shared the purpose for the changes they were making in their teaching of math. We appreciated the honesty of the staff in sharing their story. They knew it was time to spiral back and involve their learners all the way through. It was deeply encouraging to see the difference in the responses of their learners a year later.

Fast forward a couple of years and Deb is now supporting a new network school in a remote region of the Northern Territory of Australia. The focus of this school was also on mathematical understandings. She sent us an email updating us on how the work was going. Here's what she wrote:

> Yesterday Sarah and I asked the first two questions to the students and we got some great results. I just had to share the answer I got from Paul, one of the Year 4 students, in response to the question "Why is it important to learn Maths?"
>
> Paul: "So when we get big we know everything and we can help other kids and help new generations so that when we die they can have the memories."
>
> Dignity, Purpose and Options![9]

TAKE ENOUGH TIME—AND NOT TOO MUCH

You will appreciate, by this point, that scanning is not done overnight. The process can't be rushed. We often tell schools to slow down in order to speed up. What this means is that unless you take enough time in the Scanning stage to get a real sense of what is going on for your learners, you might miss the boat on some really important areas of learning. On the other hand, it is also possible to spend too long in the Scanning stage. This results in teams getting bogged down. Momentum matters.

Scans provide the overview. They are not the main event. The scans themselves initially may be somewhat imperfect. The key is to get started and to approach scanning with curiosity and with a growth-oriented mindset. During the first time through the Spiral, you might choose to limit the scanning process to a few weeks. Once the Spiral of Inquiry is integrated into school practice, scanning will become an ongoing practice.

A REMINDER ABOUT SCANNING:

Scanning Is

- Reflective of an inquiry and evidence mindset
- Genuine curiosity about what is going on for learners with a wide perspective on learning
- Finding out about what is happening for all learners by listening to them—as well as by listening to their families and their communities

Scanning Is Not

- About seeking evidence to reinforce the status quo
- Simply a focus on aspects of academic learning that are easily measured
- Exclusively about what the professionals think

BIG IDEAS FROM CHAPTER 2

- Scanning requires curiosity, open-mindedness, and actively listening to your learners.
- The two key questions from the research on social-emotional learning and metacognition are the starting point.
- Scanning is informed by an understanding of the learning sciences and enriched by knowledge of the First Peoples Principles of Learning.

FREQUENTLY ASKED QUESTIONS ABOUT SCANNING

School teams often have a lot of questions as they begin scanning. Here are some of the more common questions we hear, with some suggestions for your inquiry team to consider.

Aren't these questions too hard for young learners?

We have found that almost all learners can answer the questions if they understand the reason for them and are given enough time to think. Sometimes it works well to introduce the purpose of the questions and to have a discussion of why they are important on one day and then follow up the next day by asking the questions of individual students. Adapting the wording of the question can help, as long as the intent of the question isn't changed. For example, there is a significant difference between an adult who cares about you and an adult in the school who believes in your future success.

Who is the best person to ask the questions?

This varies depending on the context. With young children, having an adult that they know and trust works well. Often older students can be very helpful in gathering information from younger ones. Sometimes teachers have worked with learners from another class. Often formal leaders can take on a significant scaffolding role. What matters most is being clear on the *why* of the question and then figuring out the best *how* to do it for your situation.

We liked the spirit and wisdom of a Swedish educator working in an alternative setting. At the beginning of the year, she knew that her students were not yet connected to the adults in their new building. She said that she started scanning by asking each young person, "Please tell me about someone in your last school who you knew believed in you." She listened intently to the responses and then said, "I want to be that person for you here, and I am asking for your help in telling me how he made that connection with you."[10] She put the learner into the role of connectedness coach. Her strategy worked, and we were moved by her compassionate approach.

Will students take the questions seriously?

Giving learners a heads-up about the questions in a way that does not influence the answers is helpful. Students will gladly talk about what works for them—and what does not—if they believe that they will be listened to with respect. Inquiry teams who listen seriously to the learners and do the scanning process thoroughly report that they have gained powerful new insights that led to substantive change. Sharing with students the insights the team has gained will go a long way to building credibility into the process.

Could others be involved in Scanning?

Yes. Schools that include family members, support staff, and older students in the interviewing and reflecting process report important shifts in culture. As one school that included parents in a structured scanning process noted: "Parents on the team are amazingly enthusiastic about what we are doing. They are adjusting their work schedules so that they can participate. We are finding their insights and questions during the debrief are bringing a non-educator perspective that's really helping us."[11]

How long does it take?

Scanning should not be rushed, nor should it take forever. School teams usually find that four to six weeks of scanning provides enough information to move to the Focusing stage. Asking two or three important questions of learners can be done quite efficiently. As one school leader observed, "We were able to scan an entire class in about 25 minutes using a classroom teacher, support teacher, support staff person, parent, and principal team. This was followed with a debrief session of 40 minutes with the entire team where we discussed the process, considered the responses of learners, and looked for trends about what is working and what is missing. It was invaluable."

Are surveys a good way to start Scanning?

The answer is, "It depends." It depends on the purpose, the quality of the survey, the number of questions, and what you intend to do with the results. The learning and actions that came from the two questions the middle-school staff asked made a big difference over a three-month period and provided momentum for a second year of effort. We have seen students become disinterested with overly lengthy surveys. Many of you may have had the same experience when asked to respond to overly lengthy questionnaires.

Our advice is never to ask a question if you aren't prepared to act on the results. A quick survey with a few questions can provide a great deal of information. Too many questions and you may end up with an overwhelming pile of data. And, if you do decide to use a survey, then make sure that you communicate the results to your learners in a way that demonstrates you are taking their input seriously.

What about using information from local or national tests in the scanning process?

We encourage inquiry teams to look carefully at various sets of data, including those from large-scale assessments. We have found, however, that the closer the data are to the individual classroom or student, the more useful they are to the teacher. There is no substitute for talking directly with learners about whether they feel a sense of belongingness and whether they understand what they are learning and why what they are learning is important.

How do Scanning and Checking connect?

The inquiry schools that we have observed doing the deepest work ask the same questions at the end of a term, a semester, or a year to assess their progress. You want to know that every young person in your school can name at least two adults who believe in them, and you want to know that every learner understands what they are learning and why it is important. You also want to know that the key areas of concern that have emerged during scanning will become the focus for your team inquiry—and you want to know that your actions are making a difference. Scanning and checking are closely linked.

QUESTIONS FOR LEARNING CONVERSATIONS

1. Why do you think it is so important that scanning starts with listening to learners?
2. How might you use the scanning process to build curiosity amongst your colleagues?
3. Which of the learning principles—as identified by the learning sciences and by the First Peoples Principles of Learning—do you think is a strength in your school? How will you check out this assumption?
4. Similarly, which of the learning principles do you think needs more attention? How will you check this out?

LEADERSHIP MOVES

- Design simple and efficient ways to collate and share data. Use evidence that is as close as possible to the learner.
- Get directly involved in scanning. Ask the key questions yourself. Listen to a range of your learners. Share what you learn and what you are wondering.
- Model curiosity about which of the learning principles is a strength in your school and which is more of a challenge. Pick a few questions that you want to probe in more depth.
- Be open about what you are learning, hearing, wondering about.
- Don't rush.

3

FOCUSING

Deciding on Impact

Where will you concentrate your energies?
What will give you the greatest impact?

"Did you see how well Jack was able to pay attention when we were studying animal tracks outside today?" "Even though our reading results are pretty strong, it was disappointing to learn how few of our students read for pleasure." "Did you notice how much some of our kids struggle with receiving feedback?" "It was a shock to learn how few of our students understand the significance of the territorial acknowledgment." "We were pleased to hear how much our Year 7 learners are gaining from their community partners." "I was surprised to hear that Abby couldn't name a single adult in the school who believed in her. She always seems ok. I wonder what is going on."

ONCE YOU HAVE considered a range of evidence sources, and once you have listened carefully to your learners, you will have learned a lot. You will have discovered more about their sense of belongingness. You also may have a deeper understanding of the extent to which they are finding their learning purposeful, meaningful, and relevant. You will know more about their sense of agency as learners.

The scan usually leads to many new perspectives—and questions—about the experiences of learners. The challenge at the Focusing stage is to determine the areas to prioritize. This is the time to ask yourselves, "Where are we going to concentrate our efforts so that we can make a significant impact on the experiences and outcomes of our learners?"

Although it's important to get started, it's also important not to rush. The feeling of "Let's do something right away" needs to be resisted long enough to increase the odds that your actions will have the impact you want. You need to have the patience to slow down so that you can develop a deeper understanding of what is worth spending time on before moving to premature action. Investing some time in obtaining a clear focus will lead to more thoughtful actions and greater impact.

Limiting the focus to one area is highly desirable. In a comment made during the Networks of Inquiry and Indigenous Education symposium in May 2019, Helen Timperley asserted that her research shows that if you have more than one goal you probably don't have a focus.[1] An inquiry that is focused and deep, rather than scattered and shallow, helps to avoid overload and helps to build commitment. Multiple initiatives can become overwhelming and may ultimately lead to fatigue and resistance.

Nevertheless, we have seen some schools that can manage two areas of focus—context always matters. For example, in one middle school, the scan showed that many learners disliked math and their achievement was low. The staff asked themselves, "Should we focus on deepening understanding of mathematics, or should we focus on students' attitudes to mathematics?" They returned to the principles of learning and were reminded that emotions are integral to learning. They decided that attending to attitudes while deepening mathematical understandings was the way to go.

In a New Zealand school, the scanning process revealed that many learners struggled to bring voice into their writing, and they also felt disconnected from the Maori Elders in their community. This school decided to focus both on writing with strong voice and on developing community connectedness by writing for a real audience. They tackled two of the key learning principles simultaneously.

A scan in a Canadian secondary school revealed that a large number of young people were not able to provide strong answers to the key metacognitive questions, "What are you learning?" and "Why is what you are learning important?" Further scanning showed that many learners were frustrated by their assignments; they found the tasks lacked meaning and challenge. This awareness led the inquiry team to focus on assessment for learning.

These team members placed a special emphasis on clarity of intentions, so that they could make sure their students knew what they were learning and why the learning mattered. They also worked together across disciplinary boundaries to make sure that every assignment was challenging and engaging. They worked as a whole staff to make sure their assigned tasks were fewer in number, were of higher quality, and didn't result in excessive overload for learners.

DETERMINING A FOCUS—GETTING MORE EVIDENCE AND LOOKING AT STRENGTHS

At the Focusing stage, teams need to return to the central questions of the Spiral of Inquiry: "What's going on for our learners?" and "How do we know?" Once a focus is selected, there is usually a need to collect further evidence to get an even clearer picture of what is going on.

As you explore the problems and challenges in greater depth, be careful not to overlook what is working well. In every setting, there are many positive aspects for some learners. Surfacing what is working provides important information about the strengths on which to build. Understanding the challenges provides information about what to change.

By now you can see that the Spiral is not a linear process. It will have become clear that it is difficult to get a handle on what is going on for learners without asking them. It may be time for a bit more scanning. Seeking multiple ways to check with learners that you are on the right track in deciding your focus area will further strengthen commitment and understanding.

In *Leading Powerful Professional Learning*, Deirdre Le Fevre and her colleagues from the University of Auckland propose five criteria that inquiry teams will find helpful in determining the focus:

1. **Is there a sense of urgency?** The evidence says this area of focus is really important for learners.
2. **Is it good for all?** This focus will make a difference to multiple learners rather than to a select few.
3. **Do we have a critical mass?** There is a reasonable level of staff commitment.
4. **Is it manageable?** It is within the capacity of the group to tackle this area.
5. **Does it address something complex?** The focus area is a complex one that requires fresh thinking to make the changes required for learners.[2]

COMPLICATED OR COMPLEX?

A problem can be considered complicated if it can be understood by analyzing its parts and a known solution may exist to remedy it. The Spiral is designed to help school teams address the kind of complex issues for which there are currently no available answers. Tackling complex challenges requires the development of adaptive expertise. We will address the ways in which collaborative inquiry can build adaptive expertise in subsequent chapters (chapter 6 in particular). For now, however, a brief distinction between complicated and complex problems may be helpful.

According to *Leading Powerful Professional Learning*, there are some telltale signs that a problem is actually more complex than it is complicated. For example, interventions have been tried (e.g., small group instruction), but results are mixed and somewhat disappointing. Sometimes a series of workshops and classroom observations result in no observable change in practice three months later. No one can really explain why the agreed-upon changes haven't been implemented. The key point is that when dealing with people and processes, problems are often more complex than initially considered.

MAKING DECISIONS

The multiple possibilities that arise from scanning mean some potentially important areas of focus have to be set aside for a later time or handled in a way other than through intensive professional learning and collective action. One of the most difficult things for inquiry teams to do is to decide what matters the most and what can be put on hold temporarily.

Having everyone (or as close to everyone as possible) focused on what will make the most difference to learners leads to collective responsibility. When the focus is scattered, energy is dispersed, and opportunities for collective learning are diminished. A common focus generates the momentum needed to make change happen.

BUILDING IN DECISION-MAKER MOVES

A collaboration between a team of decision-making scientists—Lee Failing, Robin Gregory, and Graham Long—and inquiry leader Brooke Moore resulted in the publication of *The Decision Playbook* in 2019. This framework is designed to help educators and young people make thoughtful choices in a complex world. By applying the six decision-maker moves identified in the playbook throughout the Spiral of Inquiry—and especially at the Focusing stage—inquiry teams can make better and more thoughtful decisions about where to invest their time, energy, and resources.

Consider the following moves:

1. Frame the choice: What are we really deciding?
2. Clarify what matters: What are our objectives?
3. Generate options: How could we achieve our objectives?
4. Explore consequences: What could happen?
5. Weigh trade-offs: What's best, all things considered?
6. Stay curious: What do we need to learn or adjust?

At the Focusing stage, clarifying the values that the staff hold is especially important in shaping a decision about where to invest time and energy. An elementary staff in a suburban community identified improving students' abilities to communicate their learning and thinking as their main focus. They were also figuring out the ways to organize cohorts of learners to keep them safe during the pandemic. Before going any further, they spent a number of sessions thinking about what mattered most to them. They came up with three values, which they then used to shape their inquiry work:

- Community—we want our kids to feel cared about and supported.
- Belonging—we want our kids to feel connected to each other and to the school.
- Equity—we want our kids to know they matter and that we believe in their success.

Kate, the principal, pointed out:

> It was critical to approach our decision-making through a lens that upheld our values and continued the work towards our Spiral, and was also sensitive to students' unique needs in the throes of the pandemic. I wanted to make sure that we made the decisions in a way that honoured individual agency while ensuring that we were centred on what our learners needed.

Kate was careful about checking that their decisions matched their values and that they took the time required to do this in a thoughtful way. Clarifying values was more important than speed. We encourage teams to slow down the urge for immediate action. Nobel laureate Daniel Kahneman explains that as human beings we all use two systems of thinking. System 1 is our *fast thinking* system. Automatic, intuitive, and effortless, it produces impressions. It drives our gut reactions.

System 2 is *slow thinking*. It's what we do when we use our heads. This happens, for example, when we develop a plan, calculate something, or weigh pros and cons before choosing. Deliberate and effortful, it produces judgments.[3]

Decision scientists have identified some common traps that we can fall into when we are trying to make quick decisions. Knowing how these traps can get in the way of making better decisions at the Focusing stage can help to keep things on track. Take a look at these traps, as identified in *The Decision Playbook*. You will see that they are grouped into three main categories. Consider how these traps might trip up teams at the Focusing stage.

We stick with what we know

- We resist holding two conflicting ideas at once
- We try to confirm what we already know
- We get attached to our stories
- We do what we have always done

We take short cuts

- We anchor on the first thing
- We are swayed by what is vivid, recent, or repeated
- We oversimplify and fill in the gaps with assumptions
- We're overconfident

We hang with our crowd

- We try to conform
- We trust the people we like
- We rush to agreement
- We sometimes get more convergent thinking in groups—our views become even more restricted[4]

Disagreement is a key part of working through the Focusing stage. As *The Decision Playbook* warns:

> In all but the simplest of cases, a lack of healthy disagreement during the decision process probably means there has been insufficient attention to understanding the problem, generating creative ideas, challenging assumptions and clarifying what matters.[5]

SECONDARY SCHOOL ON THE MOVE

Here's an example from a secondary school. Mark, a new principal, had recently been appointed. The staff expressed their concerns about the lack of engagement of their Year 9 and 10 students. Their learning results were poor, and a number of them were at risk of fading out of school. The teachers did some scanning and found out that many students were unable to provide strong answers to what they were learning and why it was important.

The staff was divided about what to do next. One group was convinced that a firmer approach to discipline and more follow-up on late assignments would do the trick. Blake, an experienced and vocal member of the English department, spoke quite vehemently about how when there was a different principal, things were much better. When Blake talked, a number of his colleagues nodded their heads in silent agreement. They wanted things fixed and fixed fast. They were confident they had the answers.

Another smaller group on staff wasn't quite so sure. Andrea, the teacher librarian, wondered whether there might be more to it. Some of the staff visibly bristled at her suggestion that maybe they were part of the problem. Mark sensed a potential rift on staff and knew that a decision made in haste could lead to even greater problems. He asked the staff if they would be willing to take a little more time.

Over the next few months he supported the group interested in stronger discipline in using the decision framework to get really clear on their objectives and encouraged them to stay curious as to what options might be available. Blake started to see that by being too attached to the stories of how things used to be, he was missing the chance to make things better. Those who were interested in digging a bit deeper were encouraged to do more scanning and to report back on what they were learning. Each group was heard and respected, and trust started to grow.

By using the framework and not rushing to immediate action, the staff came to an agreement that a focus on more engaging, hands-on, nature- and community-based learning would lead to deeper engagement. Three years later, this school is in a very different place and has become a leader in place-based, cross-curricular learning. Blake is now one of the most vocal proponents of the concept of their school as a learning hub. He and Andrea are working together to develop powerful cross-curricular units of learning. The slow thinking approach that their principal encouraged helped the staff avoid the biases, traps, and assumptions that could so easily have taken them in a much less productive direction.

THINKING AHEAD TO IMPACT

Once your team has committed to a focus that is urgent, good for a majority of learners, manageable, and complex, it is time to decide how you will determine impact. What will constitute enough of a change for your learners? For example, you may have decided that your focus is to develop more intellectually engaging learning. What evidence will you look for that the students are in fact becoming stronger in that area?

If you have determined that improving oral language skills is important, what measures will give you the best information? And if you have chosen understanding and respecting different worldviews as a key area of need for your learners, how will you know your efforts are paying off?

The following questions are adapted from the work of Helen Timperley, Fiona Ell, Deidre Le Fevre, and Kaye Twyford to help you evaluate the evidence that you have decided to collect:

- What do you already have that will provide evidence of the change you want to make?
- Is what you have selected usable (accessible and readily interpreted)?
- Is what you have useful (linked to your focus area and aligned with your values)?
- What else could you collect that could be evidence of change in your context?[6]

The Focusing stage is the time for you to get clear on the changes you are looking for and—most important—figure out how you will know whether you are making *enough* of a difference for your learners.

A REMINDER ABOUT FOCUSING:

Focusing Is

- Using information from the scan to identify an area for concentrated team learning
- Gathering more information if you need it to understand the situation more fully
- Identifying strengths or positives to build on, as well as clarifying challenges
- Challenging assumptions and avoiding group think
- Identifying a complex area that requires a concerted team approach

Focusing Is Not

- The time to introduce completely new areas disconnected from the scanning process
- About assuming you have it all figured out and don't need to investigate any further
- Just about problems or challenges
- About everyone choosing their own area of interest
- About deciding quickly or picking a focus that is relatively easy to address—or one for which you already have the answer

Once the focus is clear and you know what changes you want to make for your learners, you might feel like you are ready to move to action. Not quite yet! The next step is for you to pause just a little longer to reflect on the ways in which the practices, programs, or attitudes of the adults in your school might be contributing to the situation for your learners both positively and negatively. This will take you right into the Hunch stage.

BIG IDEAS FROM CHAPTER 3

- The information you gather through the scanning process will be used to determine a focus area—a complex issue that, when addressed, will make a significant difference for your learners.
- Too many focus areas can dissipate efforts. Pick one (or two at the most).
- The decision-making framework can help clarify your choices.
- Get clear on the difference you want to make—and how you will determine the extent to which you are realizing the desired gains.

FREQUENTLY ASKED QUESTIONS ABOUT FOCUSING

How do we know when we have enough information to move to the Focusing stage?

We encourage schools to take enough time in the Scanning stage to get a good idea of what is going on for their learners. Once you start listening to learners and becoming curious about what is going on for them, you will want to know more. Scanning will become an ongoing part of your inquiry process.

Even as we encourage you to take your time, you will want to identify a focus so that within a reasonable amount of time—a term, a semester, or a year—you will be able to complete a first cycle. Our experience with schools tells us that after about six weeks of intentional scanning you will have enough information to get started on figuring out a powerful focus.

What do we do if we can't agree on a focus?

Use the criteria for selecting a focus—urgent, good for all, critical mass, manageable, and complex—to help you narrow the possibilities. Use the six decision-maker moves to frame your choices. Agree to set aside potential focus areas for future consideration. Make sure that everyone is listened to and heard before moving forward.

How will we know if our focus is complex enough?

You want to pick a focus area that requires you to learn something new, that will challenge your current thinking, and that will lead to new actions. Picking a focus where you may already have the solution and just haven't done anything about it yet does not require the kind of collaboration that the Spiral demands. For instance, if your evidence shows that learners are struggling to get along on the playground or are weak in decoding skills, there are many available strategies that can be readily applied.

Moving from decoding skills (complicated) to joy and confidence in using inferential reading skills (complex) requires new forms of expertise that the whole staff may need to develop. Tackling a new competency or capability like decision-making, creative thinking, or joint problem-solving is complex work.

Why do we need to decide the criteria for checking at the Focusing stage?

The clearer teams are on the kinds of changes they want to see in their learners, the better the chances are that those changes will be realized. Deciding the criteria at the Focusing stage will make your new learning and your new actions more intentional.

Is it acceptable to go to the Hunch stage before we determine a focus?

Yes. Often things will come up in the Scanning stage that generate a lot of internal questions and some guesses or hunches about the current situation for our learners. For instance, "What is it that we are doing that leads some learners to feel well connected and others isolated?" "Why is it that some learners thrive in some learning settings and struggle in others?" "What is leading to the drop-off in social and intellectual progress between one grade and the next?"

Going back and doing a bit more scanning, listening to learners, testing out your hunches, and getting a more complete picture of what is going on will help you to clarify your focus. The Spiral is not linear. You will go back and forth across the stages as you refine your thinking, test out your assumptions, engage in new learning, try out new actions, and check to see how much difference you are making. The key is to stay curious, stay open, and listen carefully to different voices and perspectives.

QUESTIONS FOR LEARNING CONVERSATIONS

1. Why is it so important to slow down the decision-making process at this point in the Spiral?
2. It is possible there will be different perspectives—and different priorities—among your team about what the focus area should be. How will you negotiate these differences? How might you use the decision framework to move your team to agreement?
3. How will you communicate to your learners and to your community the focus for your team inquiry? Why is it important to make adult learning visible?
4. Figuring out what evidence you will use to determine whether or not you are making a big enough difference for your learners is key at this stage. Why do you think this is so important?

LEADERSHIP MOVES

- Develop a strong personal understanding of the decision-maker moves. Practise by applying it to a decision you are currently facing.
- Listen deeply to surface a variety of viewpoints. Make sure every voice is heard.
- Model that uncertainty is part of the process. Don't leap to certainty.
- Keep coming back to the key question: "What is going to create the greatest impact for our learners?" Don't get swayed by the loudest or most dominant voices.
- Stay calm. Be patient.

4

DEVELOPING A HUNCH

Taking Responsibility

**What's leading to this situation?
How are *we* contributing to it?**

Carmella and Sanjai were bracing themselves for the start of the new year. They were to receive the class that every previous teacher said was incredibly difficult. The twenty-eight Year 6 youngsters were seen as a real handful. They were often described as boisterous, rebellious, and non-compliant. The staff had been introduced to the Spirals framework, and the two teachers decided to start the year by interviewing each of their learners. The responses to the social-emotional question were disheartening.

Very few of the students could name even one adult at the school who believed in them. Carmella and Sanjai followed up with a second question, "How would you describe yourself as a learner?" The responses took them aback.

Words like "losers," "stupid," "mean," "loud," "lazy," and "rotten" sprang from their lips. The teachers wrote down every word the students used to describe themselves and then posted the words on the staff room bulletin board. This sent a shock wave through the faculty as the staff recognized that these were the very words they had used themselves. This led the whole staff to ask, "How are we contributing to this situation?" Challenging their own assumptions led to some powerful—and positive—changes for this group of students.

As you engaged in scanning and clarified the focus for your team inquiry, we hope you heard a lot of ideas about what was going on for your learners. You may have discussed reasons for the current situation. You might have been surprised by what you learned, and you might have become even more curious about what is really going on. Your curiosity will lead you to surface a number of hunches, which takes you right into this stage of the Spiral.

When we designed the Spiral framework, we chose the word *hunch* intentionally. Hunches are based on intuition and gut instincts. Hunches may not be accurate; on the other hand, they may be right on. They do need to be checked out, however, before moving ahead too quickly. You may have had niggling feelings for a while that things could be a lot better for your learners—you just weren't sure where to start.

You may have seen some of your students struggle with making sense of a complicated text or watched others look frustrated when faced with complex problems in an inquiry project. You will have wondered why some learners seem to thrive outdoors when they are so restless in the classroom. Sometimes you might have shared your concerns with a trusted colleague, and other times you may have kept your worries to yourself.

The Hunch stage is designed to provide inquiry teams with the time and the discipline to get a deeper understanding about why things are the way they are for the learners you serve. Leaping to action without a clear understanding of the current situation for learners or without accessing new learning to inform your strategies is unlikely to produce the results that you want. The more you understand, the better informed you will be about what new actions to take. Once again, teams need to slow down the inclination to act in order to speed up the long-term impact for learners.

Team members will have all kinds of hunches about why things are the way they are. Some may hold their views passionately. Getting those strong views out on the table where everyone can talk about them is fundamental to moving forward. It can also be difficult. Challenging assumptions and biases, letting go of long-held beliefs, listening to conflicting points of view and being vulnerable in recognizing our own responsibilities are all required at this stage. One British Columbia (BC) leader describes the Hunch stage as "moving from safe spaces to brave spaces."[1] Let's take a look at some specific considerations for creating brave spaces where surfacing and testing out hunches can open up thinking.

WHERE DO *WE* HAVE CONTROL?

It's often easier to assign blame than it is to assume responsibility. Venting about the government, the district, the community, the families, the pre-schools, and the learners themselves may make us feel better temporarily. Blaming others, however, does not help us solve the problems we face. We need to look at ourselves and our practices as we ask, "How are we contributing to this situation for our learners?"

Many of us are not very good at identifying how we are contributing to particular situations. We are usually better at identifying the good things we are doing, and sometimes we are reluctant to identify the things we do that aren't helpful.

Researchers Russell Bishop, Mere Berryman, Sarah-Jane Tiakiwai, and Cath Richardson asked Maori young people what promoted or limited their learning in secondary schools. They posed the same questions to these students' teachers. The responses were startlingly different. The teacher responses contained no reference to teaching strategies. The learners, on the other hand, were able to identify a set of sophisticated learning and teaching strategies that worked for them. Many of these strategies were relationship-based. When the teachers agreed to try these culturally appropriate learning strategies—and stuck with them over time—the result was not only big learning gains but also much stronger feelings of agency and belonging.[2]

We observed one rural staff using their hunches to dramatically change their elementary language arts program. The staff was very concerned about the reading achievement of their young learners. Many of these children lived in subsidized housing, and their day-to-day conditions were often precarious. The school had introduced a school-wide guided reading approach that involved a great deal of staff commitment.

Each day started with intensive reading instruction, and yet, despite the staff's concerted efforts, reading achievement continued to lag. When teachers started the scanning process they found that few of their learners found pleasure in reading. They also discovered that many of their most vulnerable learners were often late to school and missed valuable reading time.

As the teachers surfaced their hunches, they wondered if the way they started their day was a problem. Checking with the children and their families and exploring some research about the links amongst emotions, physical activity, nutrition, and learning confirmed their hunch. The teachers shifted how they started their day. Instead of going straight to reading groups, learners started the day with dancing as a large group in the gymnasium followed by a healthy snack in their classrooms.

By the time reading sessions were about to begin, everyone was present and ready to learn. The staff restructured their reading program to make sure they had intriguing books widely available, and they adopted a series of thoughtful new strategies.[3]

The parents were happier too, especially since they were invited to have coffee and snacks after they dropped off their children. They no longer felt they were being judged negatively if their child was a few minutes late or if their child struggled with reading.

Over a period of two years this school showed impressive gains in reading. The children in this school now not only read well—they are enjoying it. Having the courage to examine their own practices and to check out their hunches led this school staff to make critically important changes. After they consolidated their literacy strategies, they began serious work on the competency of creative thinking with an active arts and design initiative.

As a result of their thorough scanning, a small secondary school in northern BC focused on creating a greater sense of belonging and connection for their

Indigenous learners. They planned to incorporate lessons and resources that were more culturally relevant and to develop stronger home-school connections. While the staff was committed to the direction, it took some challenging conversations at the Hunch stage to explore why their Indigenous learners felt disconnected from the school and from the curriculum.

Many teachers acknowledged that they felt ill-equipped to infuse Indigenous understandings into the curriculum. Their lack of knowledge and understandings of Indigenous history, culture, and ways of knowing were impeding their progress. They struggled to make connections with the families and were uncomfortable acknowledging the generational trauma that existed in their community.

By surfacing the ways in which their own doubts, fears, and lack of knowledge were holding them back, this staff became ready to take some giant steps forward. Two years later the impact in this school—and the community—is tangible. As one of the teachers said, "Spending the time to build relationships and a sense of community is not taking time away from the curriculum—it is the curriculum. Our Indigenous students are now raising topics to discuss and are proud to share their culture."

Surfacing hunches about our own behaviours, attitudes, assumptions, beliefs, programs, and structures can be the starting point for significant change.

RESPECTING AND TESTING HUNCHES

Having open and honest conversations about what may be leading to specific situations for learners is essential. These conversations must be conducted in a respectful manner. Dismissing another's views as uninformed or inaccurate without first seeking to understand is disrespectful and will erode trust. You need to be open to having your assumptions challenged. When our assumptions go unquestioned, we can start to believe that the assumptions we hold are the truth.

One of the challenges in surfacing hunches is that they are often passionately held to be the "truth," when they are really just an assumption or a perception. These "truths" are often about other people and come out in expressions such as "They won't ..." or "If only they would ...." While it might be tempting to ignore or dismiss these opinions, you do so at the risk of eroding trust and respect. When there are deeply held beliefs about reasons for the current situation, it is important to check them out in some way and then look at the implications for your own behaviour.

Adam Grant, in his book *Think Again,* suggests that too many of us favour "the comfort of conviction over the discomfort of doubt."[4] He contends that intelligence is traditionally viewed as the ability to think and learn, "yet, in a turbulent world, there's another set of cognitive skills that might matter more: the ability to rethink and unlearn."[5] The Hunch stage requires teams to rethink what is considered to be the truth.

In conducting research on literacy improvement, Helen Timperley and a group of colleagues were engaged in a conversation at a primary school. The staff were adamant that the reason literacy achievement was low was that families were sending their children to school without breakfast. The proposed change strategy was to provide food. It would have been easy for the research team to dismiss this suggestion. Instead, they asked the staff to check with the learners and their families about what they had for breakfast.

Within a few days, the staff learned that in almost every home, children had access to nutritious local food. It just wasn't the standard western fare of bacon and eggs or cereal. Once this hunch had been checked out, the staff were much more willing to consider other possibilities, including specific inferential literacy strategies.

Some schools develop agreements about *how* they will discuss learning and teaching issues. These agreements, or norms, can help rebuild relationships in cultures where trust has been eroded. In one secondary school we visited recently, the staff felt disconnected from the vision and the school improvement plans. For some years the principal had decided on the goals, written the plan, and communicated it directly to the parent group and the district. Trust was low, resentment was high, and little engaged student learning was visible.

When that principal retired, Sebastian was assigned to the school. This new leader, who had a very open style, wanted to create a more inquiry-oriented culture, and he encouraged teachers to develop an agreement about how they would talk with one another when they began their professional conversations. The staff was skeptical at first, but a few teacher-leaders stepped forward and said they would give it a try.

At the end of two hour-long sessions, the teachers agreed that in future professional conversations they would:

- Listen without interruption to understand what was being said by the person speaking
- Ask clarifying questions
- Respectfully probe to check accuracy of hunches, perceptions, or assumptions
- Share their ideas as one possibility ("a suggestion I have is ...")
- Welcome feedback as an opportunity to learn

Developing norms about how to surface hunches and talk with one another created the beginning of a culture shift. The school staff is currently exploring strategies to help every learner be more metacognitively empowered, and they are using *Developing Self-Regulating Learners* by Deborah L. Butler, Leyton Schnellert, and Nancy E. Perry as an anchor text for their professional learning sessions. Their new norms for decision-making are helping them become a more powerful learning organization.

Australian author Joan Dalton, in her *Learning Talk* series, provides a valuable set of resources for school teams interested in developing the kinds of conversational skills that build trust and open up thinking. She observes that "When you respectfully probe and challenge assumptions, you help to bring about the intellectual discomfort or dissonance necessary for learning to take place."[6] As she emphasizes repeatedly, the key stance is *respectful*.

Here are a few questions from her work that you might find useful as you talk about your hunches:

Clarify

- Can you explain a bit more about ...?
- Can you help me understand what you mean when you say ...?
- I am curious to know more about ...?

Probe

- What do you believe?
- What might be a concrete example of this?
- Given your experience in this area, how would this work?

Explore different perspectives

- How might someone else view this?
- What other perspectives might need to be considered?
- I wonder what your students (and/or their family members) might say?

LEARNING, RISK-TAKING, AND VULNERABILITY

Learning is part of every stage of the Spiral. Scanning requires us to learn by looking at evidence broadly and by listening to learners. At the Focus stage, we learn to make decisions and set priorities. And now at the Hunch stage, we need to learn to take responsibility for our part in what is going on for our learners.

In "Looking Back and Moving Forward: Where to Next for Networks of Learning?" Alan Daly and Louise Stoll suggest that we need to consider the importance of "moving from a community of learners to become a community that learns—a subtle but important difference."[7] Careful handling of the discussions at the Hunch stage can be key to the growth of a staff, as this stage often requires having honest dialogues about issues that are simmering below the surface.

These researchers point out:

> High-trust contexts support greater willingness for individuals to be vulnerable with one another in sharing areas of difficulty and challenge. To move educators forward in the current space, we must embrace the vulnerability it takes to be open and put the other ahead of ourselves. If we want to understand what is at the core of building networks, it is vulnerability and a willingness to take risks. Equity, innovation, improving practice, change, and relationships all require a level of vulnerability. Allowing ourselves, and supporting the conditions for others to feel safe, is job one for change and growth.[8]

At this stage in the Spiral, someone needs to have the courage to put the first hunch on the table. This can require a high degree of vulnerability. We were impressed several years ago by the work in a small elementary school. The teachers had identified that their learners were struggling with inferential reading. Months later, they were no further ahead. The breakthrough came when one experienced teacher said during a meeting, "I really don't know how to read inferentially myself, let alone how to teach it."

This led to a collective sigh of relief as one after another, teachers confessed their lack of confidence in their own meaning-making abilities let alone their capacity to develop their readers. This insight motivated them to engage in new professional learning based on Ellin Keene and Susan Zimmerman's *Mosaic of Thought*. They then developed a creative cross-grade approach to reading instruction and comprehension. The innovative work of this school attracted hundreds of visiting teachers over the next few years. The young readers became so good at discussing their reading with each other that their work was highlighted in Lorna M. Earl and Helen Timperley's book *Professional Learning Conversations: Challenges in Using Evidence for Improvement*.

Formal leaders have a key role in ensuring that teachers feel safe in discussing how their professional practices may be impacting the experiences of their learners. In chapter 2 we referred to an elementary school where the scan seemed to point the team to a school-wide focus on anxiety reduction through mindfulness training. It was at the Hunch stage that the leadership team encouraged the group to take two additional weeks to look more closely at what was going on.

It was a breakthrough moment when two teachers fielded their hunch: "I wonder if the way we are giving feedback in our math program is contributing to the anxiety of our students?" The teachers agreed to interview three students each and to report back at their next meeting. When they met again and examined what the learners had to say, they realized there was strong evidence that their hunch was accurate.

What were their next steps? They developed a focus that combined math problem-solving strategies with formative feedback designed to build learner confidence. School-wide they taught the metaphor of the learning pit, where you first have to "go down" into the pit to grapple with learning issues before you climb up to higher levels of understanding.[9] The results? Two years later they were a demonstration school for growth mindset and formative assessment in math. Student anxiety had been replaced with confidence.

In a small northern BC school, teachers observed that learners routinely became frustrated by difficult tasks. They immediately resorted to asking for help from the teacher and often simply gave up. Initially the inquiry team decided that assessment for learning would be their focus. It was at the Hunch stage, however, that the team recognized that it wasn't just their assessment strategies that needed to change.

The case study from this school illustrates the insights that the teachers were able to share when the inquiry team provided the safety to do so:

> We shouldn't just expect them to persevere if they haven't been taught strategies that would take them through challenges. We also recognized that the language we adults were using in classrooms and around the school might be contributing to fixed mindsets. We needed to learn more effective ways of teaching this and we needed to develop our own mindfulness around the words we choose to use with our learners.[10]

By acknowledging that their classrooms were not always safe environments for student risk-taking, this staff became ready to dive into learning more about the impact of mindsets. Their work over the next couple of years led to significant growth in their learners. As one parent reported, "I have noticed that he has determination and a great positive outlook even if he attempts something new and fails. I heard him saying 'not just yet but one day soon.' It's fantastic."

VULNERABILITY AND RISK RESEARCH

Researchers Helen Timperley, Fiona Ell, Deirdre Le Fevre, and Kaye Twyford from the University of Auckland have explored teacher vulnerability in depth. In their work on risk, emotions, uncertainty, and vulnerability, they observed that the stance taken by inquiry leadership teams at the Hunch stage makes a big difference. They suggest that leaders recognize that emotions and motivation are intertwined:

> It is not enough to just acknowledge risk—having acknowledged it, effective leaders take action to reduce perceptions of risk, decrease uncertainty and make vulnerability an acceptable, positive and important aspect of engaging in change.[11]

Creating a space for safety and vulnerability builds motivation, trust, and commitment. Vulnerability—admitting that we don't know everything or that we are unsure about what to do—must not be seen as a weakness. In fact, it should be seen as real courage. As leadership researcher Brené Brown states in *Daring Greatly*:

> Vulnerability is not weakness, and the uncertainty, risk and emotional exposure we face every day are not optional. Our only choice is a question of engagement. Our willingness to own and engage with our vulnerability determines the depth of our courage and the clarity of our purpose.[12]

We see the Hunch stage as the place where we grow collectively as a profession. We take a close look at ourselves and the impact of our actions, we listen carefully to others, we challenge our assumptions, we demonstrate our willingness to take risks, and we engage in important, significant conversations.

Lean into the Hunch stage and don't skip over it. As a leadership team, you will create spaces for brave conversations, and you will be ready to challenge assumptions. You will have your own assumptions challenged, you will listen with respect, and you will check out hunches for accuracy. Done well, the Hunch stage will not only bring greater clarity and commitment to your focus area but will also contribute to your school being a community that learns. If you belong to a network of schools, the whole community can learn from your experiences.

So, what happened with Carmella and Sanjai's class? After they got over their shock at what their learners had to say, they knew things had to change. Because the majority of this class was boys (24 of 28 students), they dove into the research on boys and their learning. They made "making school a place where boys can thrive" the focus of their inquiry. They found a book by Barry MacDonald about strategies for boys particularly helpful and they immersed themselves in learning more about hands-on, project-based learning. They also paid attention to the girls in the class, and they found they appreciated the action-oriented strategies as well.

They paired their class up with the incoming kindergarten class and, over the course of the year, the Year 6 group designed and built an imaginative playground and a construction site for use by the younger children. In the process, they learned math, language arts, science, design, leadership, communication, collaboration, and social skills.

This class acquired a new identity as leaders both in the school and in their small town. At the end of the year they were asked to help organize the annual community fair and lead a parade through the village. By listening to these young people, challenging their own assumptions about the situation, and then taking informed action, Carmella and Sanjai had set this group of young learners on a significantly different trajectory—losers no more. At their local network celebration, they were able to report with confidence that their whole town had a much more positive view of their school.

A REMINDER ABOUT DEVELOPING A HUNCH:

Developing a Hunch Is

- Getting deeply held beliefs and assumptions out on the table about your own practices that are contributing to the situation for your learners
- Focusing on things your team can do something about
- Checking your assumptions for accuracy before moving ahead

Developing a Hunch Is Not

- A general brainstorm of all possibilities
- Being obsessed with the actions of others or with issues over which you have limited influence
- Venting about the past, fuming about the present, or finding someone to blame

We hope by now that you have seen that the Spiral is an iterative, back-and-forth process. You might start with a hunch, then do some scanning, determine a focus, scan some more, and surface even more hunches. Or you might start with learning something new and then becoming curious about the extent to which this is part of the lived experience of your learners. Regardless of the starting point, new learning is a critical part of the process. That's where we will go next.

BIG IDEAS FROM CHAPTER 4

- The Hunch stage requires us to look at our own practices, attitudes, and assumptions and take responsibility for the ways in which we are contributing to the situation—good or bad—for our learners.
- Hunches are not necessarily correct. Hunches must be treated with respect and checked out for accuracy.

- Conversations at the Hunch stage can be challenging and require skilled facilitation by the leadership team. Leaders often need to make themselves vulnerable first.

FREQUENTLY ASKED QUESTIONS ABOUT THE HUNCH STAGE

Why is it so important that the hunches are about teacher practices or school-wide approaches?

We can lose a lot of energy fretting or fuming about things over which we have limited control. The Spiral of Inquiry is about making differences for learners, and this means changing teacher practices and designing new approaches as a team. Without a good understanding of how our current practices are affecting our learners, we can miss the opportunity to have a big impact. The more we place our energy in places where we have influence (i.e., our own practices), the greater our sphere of influence becomes.

What can the leadership team do to build trust at the Hunch stage?

Inquiry leaders build trust by developing thoughtful spaces for the hard conversations that are required. Listening respectfully, creating norms for dialogue, and bringing a spirit of genuine curiosity to this stage by exploring hunches rather than brushing them off will help to build trust. Leaders who show their vulnerability by surfacing hunches about their own practices and behaviours help to create safe spaces for others to do so as well.

What if the team needs to do more scanning after surfacing some hunches?

Then scan some more! The Spiral is not a straight line or a set of tick boxes. It is more than likely that issues will be raised during the Hunch stage that will require some further exploration. By checking out your hunches with your learners—and by sharing your hunches with them—you will be creating a genuine community of learners. Spend the time you need to make sure you are on the right track. Just avoid spending so much time that you lose momentum.

What if our hunches seem to be more about what we *could* do than what we are doing?

This is natural. Our inclination as teachers is that once we understand a problem, we want to fix it right away. As the leadership team, simply bring the conversation back to raising your own hunches about why things are the way they are. It's important to avoid the temptation to leap to action, and you don't want to stifle enthusiasm. The Hunch stage is about really understanding what is going on right now. Moving to action will come soon enough. We want to make sure that our actions are informed by the most current and relevant research. This is why the New Professional Learning stage, which comes next, is so important.

QUESTIONS FOR LEARNING CONVERSATIONS

1. How will you create the conditions where there is enough psychological safety for teachers to surface their hunches?
2. To what extent do you think an agreement on norms for discussion would be helpful in your setting? How will you go about establishing these norms?
3. What does vulnerability mean to you? Why is it important for leaders to express their own vulnerability?
4. How will you keep the discussion focused on understanding the current situation for your learners and avoid moving to solutions too quickly? Why is this important?

LEADERSHIP MOVES

- Co-create a set of norms for team conversations. Stick to the guidelines yourself.
- Consider taking the first step. Put your own hunches out on the table. Test them out and be prepared to be wrong.

5

NEW PROFESSIONAL LEARNING

The Importance of Informed Action

Ann Marie and her colleagues at a large urban elementary school had observed that their students, many of whom came from refugee families, had some gaps in their learning. The staff had surfaced a number of hunches about the ways in which the programs at the school contributed positively and negatively to developing learner agency. They realized that many of their learners had a limited connection to their new place and that, as their teachers, they had a limited understanding of who each young person was as a learner. The staff was committed to the core competencies in their new curriculum, and they wanted to help develop a strong sense of positive personal and cultural identity.

The inquiry team wondered if spending more time learning in and from nature would help increase self-regulation. They were interested in developing a deeper understanding of the culture of the local Indigenous people. They wanted to help their learners create a greater sense of identity and connection. As a group, the team realized they needed to learn much more about the Indigenous stories of their community. They also had a lot to learn about how to take learning outside in a densely populated urban environment. They wondered how and where to begin with their new areas of professional learning.

AT THIS POINT in the Spiral, you too will have done a lot of scanning. In addition, you will have listened to your learners, and you will have used the decision framework to help you identify one or two key areas of focus. Because you have asked the two key questions, you have crucial information about your learners' sense of belonging and the extent to which they have internalized the big ideas that you have decided are important for them to learn.

You will have considered the extent to which the experiences of your learners reflect the learning principles from western and Indigenous perspectives (see chapter 2). You have had some important conversations with your inquiry team colleagues about what is leading to the current situation for your learners. Now it's time to figure out your next steps. This is the time to ask yourselves, "How and where can we learn more about what to do?"

It isn't enough for leadership teams to determine what new learning is required. It is also essential that you consider how you will organize professional learning to meet the needs of all the adults on your staff. These are big questions, and for this reason we have divided the New Professional Learning stage into two chapters. In this chapter we will provide some suggestions about the *what* of new learning and in the following chapter we will explore some ideas about the *how* of designing new learning.

The possibilities for new learning are endless. In many ways, professional development is a big industry. The number of online resources, reference books, workshops, conferences, webinars, Twitter talks, podcasts, and experts to choose from can be daunting. Fortunately for inquiry leadership teams, we have

Helen Timperley's work to guide our decisions. In 2007, she and her research colleagues at the University of Auckland produced a synthesis of the best evidence on teacher professional learning, entitled *Teacher Professional Learning and Development: Best Evidence Synthesis (BES)*. This work was ground-breaking in the clarity of its focus. The research team searched for evidence about teacher professional learning that actually made a difference to learner outcomes. Given the enormous sums of money invested annually in teacher professional development, it seemed about time that this evidence was sought.

One of the central and disturbing findings from this study was that in many parts of the world, much professional development was based on whatever set of ideas had prominence at the moment, rather than on the specific learning needs of young people. Unfortunately, this is still the case in too many schools and systems.

This chapter is designed to help your inquiry team think about the links between what you are discovering about your learners and what more you need to learn so that they can thrive. We encourage you to think about the core competencies that are shaping curriculum revisions in many parts of the world. What is it that you and your team need to learn if you have identified communication skills, social awareness and responsibility, critical thinking, or collaboration as your focus? What are some approaches to new learning, linked to the major scanning questions based on the western principles of learning identified by the Organisation for Economic Co-operation and Development (OECD) and the First Peoples Principles of Learning (FPPL), that will make a big difference to your learners?

It would be impossible for us to catalogue all the approaches and resources that you might consider. What we can offer, however, is a perspective on new learning and some specific areas of learning that the inquiry-oriented schools with which we are connected have found helpful. These include:

1. **Social-emotional learning and connectedness.** If your scanning revealed, as it has in many schools, that there are learners who do not feel a sense of connection and belonging and who cannot name at least two adults in the building who believe in their potential, then a focus on social-emotional learning is a must. The importance of a sense of belonging and the connections between emotions and motivation are well documented. We like the emphasis in one

British Columbia (BC) elementary school where the focus over two years has been caring for self, caring for others, and caring for place. In many schools, this emphasis has become the starting point for significant change.

2. **Assessment for learning and learner agency.** If learners are unable to say in their own words what they are learning and why it is important, it is highly unlikely that they are intellectually engaged. The inability to make a connection between the big ideas in the curriculum and their lives outside school underlines the importance of communicating clear learning intentions. Lack of confidence in describing how they are doing and the inability to articulate the next steps in their learning is an indicator that more work needs to be done on formative assessment and self-regulated learning strategies.

3. **Inquiry-based learning at the classroom and whole-school levels.** Your scanning may have revealed that there was a lack of opportunity for learners to explore topics in depth or to see the relevance of their assignments. You may have shared your concerns that (consistent with much of the research on curiosity in schools) instead of curiosity increasing amongst your learners, the quality and quantity of questions they raise actually seems to be diminishing over time.

   A few years ago, we had a conversation with the admissions officer at a prestigious British university. He said that every young person applying to his university was at or near the top of their class based on academic achievement. High marks did not distinguish one applicant from another. What his university was looking for were young people who had sustained interest over time in a topic of significance to them. It didn't matter whether this was model trains, chess, astronomy, horticulture, or world religions. What mattered most was the depth of curiosity and the capacity to sustain interest over time. Leaders in many organizations and institutions have realized that inquiry-based learning in depth can become the spark for the kind of curiosity that drives learning for a lifetime. Curiosity is not just for the elite.

4. **Place-based learning and Indigenous understandings.** Place-based education relies on using place—including lands and water, people and organizations, history, culture, and community—as a starting point for learning. Perhaps

your scanning revealed, as in the case of Ann Marie's school, that many of your learners know very little about their own community or about the land on which their schools and homes are located.

Maybe you found that your learners are concerned about the environment and climate change but feel powerless to do anything about it. Maybe you were struck by the importance of the First Peoples Principle of Learning that "Learning ultimately supports the well-being of the self, the family, the community, [and] the land."[1] If your focus is on creating a greater sense of community and of connection to the land, then learning more about place-based learning and teaching may be where you choose to start.

Each of these focus areas is important—and you can't do everything at once. We got a real kick out of it when Helen Timperley, a serious scholar, used a YouTube clip from Sesame Street to make the point that you can't learn a new skill if you are intent on hanging on to an old one.[2] *Putting Down the Duckie* (of old practices) can become a helpful reminder as you move into the New Professional Learning stage of the Spiral.

We have seen the impact where school teams are clear on their overall focus and are prepared to start small. As teams spiral deeper with their own learning, these small changes can amount to significant transformations in the experiences of their learners and in the cultures of their schools.

This chapter will emphasize the importance of new professional learning at this stage in the Spiral, and then take a slightly deeper dive into the specific areas listed above and how they connect directly to the key scanning questions. In the following chapter we will share some perspectives on quality teacher professional learning, the connection between the Spiral and the development of adaptive expertise, and some observations about the need to pay attention to teacher developmental stages.

THE CASE FOR NEW PROFESSIONAL LEARNING AS A SPIRAL STAGE

At one point while we were conceptualizing the Spiral process, we had an animated discussion with Helen Timperley about whether "new learning" needed to be a distinct stage. She said that the Spiral was *all* about new professional learning. We agreed. Yet we also believed, and still do, that it is essential to have a specific point in the Spiral where inquiry teams slow down to ask themselves, "What more do we need to learn, and how will we access that knowledge?" Better outcomes for learners are realized when educators acquire new knowledge and develop new skills that lead to new actions. Without new professional learning, you run the risk of falling into the trap of doing what you have always done and hoping for better outcomes. This approach is not only delusional but also demoralizing. We concluded that new professional learning was simply too important to be left to chance.

There is a lot to think about when determining what more you need to learn. You need to consider the content of your new learning and also determine *how* it will be introduced and applied in your context. Sometimes inquiry teams move quickly to introducing new programs and strategies without the whole staff having a clear understanding of the theory behind the program or strategy. This can lead to reduced impact. Professional learning can also be derailed by leaping to what is convenient, expedient, readily available, or popular. Occasionally, someone in a position of authority, disconnected from the school, decides what and how teachers are to learn. This doesn't build commitment or ownership. Many teachers justifiably resist the imposition of external directives because they have not been part of either the analysis of evidence or the decision-making process.

Changing practice in deeply informed ways involves new learning of both theory and strategies. Teachers need to know *why* the new practice is more powerful than what they have done before. This is the theory part. Yet understanding the reason for changing practice is insufficient without knowing what changes to make, so you also need to consider *how* the changes will be introduced and adapted to your context. This is the practice part.

Wise, strong, and new ways

Wise ways

When we wrote the original *Spirals of Inquiry: For Equity and Quality* in 2013, we encouraged educators to consider weaving three ways of learning—wise, strong, and new—into their practices. We believe that drawing from the wisdom traditions informed by rich Indigenous learning practices will benefit all learners. We encourage the use of contemporary research evidence to guide us toward practices that have a demonstrated impact on student learning. And we encourage you to stay open to emergent knowledge that will lead to more innovative approaches.

During our discussion of the Scanning stage in chapter 2, we invited you to consider the First Peoples Principles of Learning and to be curious about the extent to which these principles were reflected in the experiences of your learners. These principles, rooted in Indigenous traditions, apply to all learners and to all forms of learning in every community. As Tsun Dax Laura Tait, a respected Indigenous leader in BC, stated emphatically at the Networks of Inquiry and Indigenous Education (NOIIE) symposium on May 3, 2014, "What is good for Indigenous learners is good for ALL learners."

Our own experiences in listening more carefully, in exploring our own family stories, in being part of respectful intergenerational learning communities, and in encouraging nature-based learning have underlined just how relevant the First Peoples Principles of Learning are throughout a lifetime. We hope you see these connections as well.

Dr. Lorna Wanosts'a7 Williams from the Lílwat Nation is the former Canada Research Chair in Indigenous Knowledge and Learning at the University of Victoria.[3] Her contributions to Indigenous education and her advocacy for Indigenous language revitalization programs have been recognized nationally and internationally. We feel deeply fortunate to have worked with her and to have her consider us as friends. Among the many lessons we have learned from this leader is the power of language. There are terms in the Lílwat language that capture aspects of learning that we have all experienced, and yet we don't have the equivalent words for in English. Here are a few examples:

Cwelelep—being in a place of dissonance; uncertainty in anticipation of new learning; to spin like a dust storm. We all feel the excitement in the pit of our stomachs when we are on the verge of doing something we want to do[,] but it is new and we aren't sure we can master it, like pushing off the first time going solo on a bicycle. When we are learning [something new,] we need to make friends with that energy, make use of it to do what is new to us and to get past our fear of the unknown and our feelings of inadequacy.

Kamúcwkalha—the felt energy indicating group alignment and the emergence of a common group purpose. A group is ready to work together, to listen to one another and speak without fear.

Kat'íl'a—finding stillness and quietness amid our busyness and need to know; learning to keep oneself calm is necessary on the land and living in close quarters with a large group of people.[4]

Strong ways

We are fortunate as educators to have access to a wealth of formal research studies about what makes a difference to learners and their learning. There is powerful evidence regarding how young people learn particular subject matters, how to promote intrinsic motivation and social-emotional learning, and what contributes to high levels of intellectual engagement.

We must not ignore this evidence base. We have been known to say that ignoring the research evidence on what makes a difference to learners and their learning is the educational equivalent of malpractice. These are strong words and we believe them.

The seven learning principles from the Centre for Educational Research and Innovation (CERI)'s study on innovative learning environments (chapter 2) reflect contemporary understandings about what is required for deeper learning. This is why we invited you to use the learning principles as a window into the experiences of your learners during the scanning process. These principles also have implications for the New Professional Learning stage.

As you have scanned what is going on for your learners, you may have found that some of these principles are a regular part of the lived experiences of your learners. You may also have discovered that there are other principles that are experienced less frequently—or not at all. Simply understanding that it is important to stretch all learners does not tell you what this might look like for your specific learners or how to do it.

Context also matters. Building horizontal connections with the community, creating greater connectivity across subject areas, and developing strong nature-based learning will look different depending on your community, your culture, and your circumstances. Connections with community may look very different in Mayo[5] than in Madrid.

New ways

The CERI study on innovative learning environments (2009–17) was designed to surface and build on innovative practices that reflected the best of what was currently known about learning and teaching. The submitted case studies provided a rich array of strategies and initiatives that provided some substantive prompts for discussion and action within the graduate programs that we have taught at Vancouver Island University and at the University of British Columbia. For instance, an innovative land-based initiative developed in Israel was adapted by a small rural school in northern BC. The researchers in Israel and the young learners in BC were able to share their experiences and their results through videoconferencing. This is just one small example of the myriad ways in which technology is shaping the experiences of learners.

Since the completion of the CERI study, advances in technology have continued to grow exponentially. While new technologies have often been held out as the answer to educational problems (probably since the invention of the printing press), the current proliferation of hand-held devices, the increasing access to broadband internet, and the explosion in social media are creating unprecedented opportunities for new ways of learning.

The pandemic has accelerated the use of technology, even for the most reluctant of users. As memories of the pandemic fade, many of these new ways will stick. Capturing all of the ways in which technology is shaping teaching and learning is far beyond the scope of this book. What we would like to describe, however, are three recent examples that show the capacity of technology to change learning experiences at a national, global, and very personal level.

We have been fortunate to be part of the Brookings Institution study on family engagement during the COVID-19 pandemic. Over forty jurisdictions across six continents were involved in this study, and much discussion focused on the ways in which technology is being used to create community and provide quality remote learning. Many of the examples reflect the creativity and resilience of educators and families facing enormous challenges.

Consider the situation in Botswana, with half a million students in mostly small rural communities. The Young 1ove organization developed and trialled a low-tech solution using SMS messages and phone calls to provide educational instruction for students in ten thousand households across Botswana. They ran rapid randomized trials that produced some of the first experimental evidence on minimizing the fallout of the pandemic on learning. Their results showed that "remote instruction by phone and simple SMS texts can reduce innumeracy by up to 52% for less than $14 per child."[6] Furthermore, "over 99% of parents reported demand for continued remote learning services even if schools reopened."[7] We share this as an example of the ways in which new—and not necessarily high-tech—approaches can have a profound impact.

A second example comes from the work at Lyfta,[8] an immersive learning platform designed to nurture resilience, empathy, and global citizenship. Founder and filmmaker Serdar Ferit's dream is to create a storyworld from every one of the 195 countries in the world. The storyworlds provide the opportunity for students to explore real-life stories through 360° environments. Each storyworld features a genuine human story selected to spark curiosity, compassion, and empathy. We have viewed—and have been moved by—these stories.

Finally, on a personal level, we have seen—from our granddaughter's Grade 1 class—how a thoughtful educator can build a broader community on a daily basis by using the power of photographs, artifacts, and short videos to share real-time learning with family members on a weekly basis. In addition to sharing insights into the classroom, this teacher has also involved her students in developing compassion and social responsibility through her initiative Everybody Deserves a Smile.[9] We have all benefitted from her wisdom.

As you begin to determine the content and direction for your new learning, we invite you to consider the ways in which you are weaving wise, strong, and new ways into your own practice. Are you drawing on traditions that have stood the test of time over hundreds of generations? Are you looking to the current evidence base about what has been demonstrated to have a strong impact on learning? Are you staying open to new understandings about the ways in which new conceptions about time, space, relationships, technology, community, curriculum, and place are leading to promising new practices? Are you staying sensitive to the particular context of your school and the needs of your learners? Are you looking within your school for strengths you can draw on? And are you also looking outside your school and your community to discover innovative practices that can inform your own actions?

New learning connected to the key questions

We asked you to start the Spiral process by asking some key questions: "Can you name two adults who believe you will be a success in life? Can you describe how they show you that they believe in you?" and "What are you learning? And why is it important?"

The reason for asking these questions is connected to the absolute necessity that *every* learner be confident that there are educators in their schools who have their backs. Furthermore, for learners to be intellectually engaged (and for learning to truly be at the centre of all that we do in schools) we need to make sure that *every* learner knows what they are learning and why that learning is important.

Two dimensions connected to these questions come from the social-emotional repertoire and from theory and practice regarding assessment for learning. Let's take a brief look at how learning more in each of these domains can help strengthen connectedness, engagement, and agency.

SOCIAL-EMOTIONAL LEARNING AND CONNECTEDNESS

Andy Hargreaves and Dennis Shirley in their 2021 book, *Well-Being in Schools*, suggest that COVID-19 turned our assumptions about what matters in schools and society upside down.[10] They argue that a focus on well-being must become a priority. They ask, "rather than teaching kids only how to perform or produce, why can't we also teach them how to be and how to live together as human beings?"[11]

The research about the importance of social-emotional learning (SEL) is compelling.[12] The links among emotion, motivation, and school success have been described in a number of research studies and articles,[13] and there is no doubt about the importance of student connectedness and sense of belonging. And yet, at the beginning of the Spiral process, very few schools in our experience have reported that *every* learner could name two adults who believed in them and provide detailed descriptions about how the adults let them know they believed in them.

We did find one school where this was the case, and we were curious about what led to this outcome. We discovered that the school had been involved for several years in applying the Learning in Depth model.[14] In this approach to imaginative education, learners have the opportunity to explore an individual topic in depth and over time. The leadership team had worked hard to build a culture where caring and curiosity were central for both adults and students. Each learner at this school felt known and valued for their unique knowledge. The key message from this school is that a sense of belonging is connected to involving learners in deeply purposeful learning.

Being, belonging, becoming

For the past few years in BC, we have been fortunate to support an initiative designed to improve transitions for Indigenous learners. The participating schools are using the Spiral of Inquiry process to determine what is going on for their learners and then to work together to improve the experiences of young people as they move through periods of change in their schooling.[15]

This work has been influenced by the research of Kate Tilleczek, who documented the issues related to student transition from elementary to secondary school in countries including Canada, the UK, Aotearoa/New Zealand, and the US. She suggests that adults consider the concepts of *being*, *belonging*, and *becoming* as guiding principles for thinking about the transitions that youth make in their lives.[16]

For us, *being* refers to the sense of identity of the young person. Are they known and valued for who they are? Are they developing a strong sense of personal identity? The importance of *belonging* has been highlighted in the OECD publication "The Future of Education and Skills":

> A sense of belonging is relevant for 2030 because as tasks and problems become more complex, and goals more uncertain, undefined and ambiguous in the world, students must have a sense of belonging to the larger society that instils within them an obligation to contribute to the well-being of society.[17]

A 2021 report by Kaleen Healey and Chloe Stroman states that "belonging is a universal human need that is fundamentally linked to learning" and well-being. Belonging "describes an individual's experience of feeling that they are, or are likely to be, accepted and respected as a valued contributor in a specific environment."[18] Moreover, "When students experience a sense of belonging in a learning environment there are both immediate and long-term positive consequences for their academic performance and well-being."[19] A sense of belonging to the greater society starts with a feeling of belonging and connection to the school community. Finally, the idea of *becoming* draws attention to the developmental aspects of learning and change. Do learners see themselves as becoming more competent, more skilled, and more confident as a result of their schooling experiences?

Sadly, there are still too many learners who do not feel known and valued in their schools. These young people do not feel a sense of belonging, and they struggle to find the relevance in what they are asked to do and learn. It is only by asking questions—and listening with open hearts and minds—that these disconnected and disengaged learners can be identified. Once we know better, then we can move to more informed action.

We also need to be careful with our assumptions. A school might offer a range of activities and pride itself on its caring culture and therefore assume that every learner feels a sense of belonging and is able to name the adults who believe in their future success. Teachers may have gone out of their way to ensure their learners have access to food, clothing, and supplies. And even in these caring spaces, we have seen educators surprised by the answers they hear when young people are asked specifically to name the actions of the adults that demonstrate their belief in their future success.

Previously we introduced you to the strategy of the 2 x 10 where an adult in the school commits to talking to a disconnected learner for two minutes a day for ten days in a row about a topic that has nothing to do with school (see chapter 2).

In Ontario, where for several years the province invested heavily in secondary school success, this strategy was used widely. Michael Fullan reports in his book *Stratosphere* that the wide use of the 2 x 10 dialogue was successful in getting a large proportion of learners on a better path toward graduation.

Stratosphere also describes the work of American researcher Susan Nolen. At a major research conference, she described what happened when teachers were asked to spend thirty minutes of out-of-class time (for instance over lunch hour or during an extracurricular activity) getting to know a student with whom they had not been connecting. The teachers overwhelmingly said that using this simple strategy not only gave them a deeper and more positive understanding of the young person but often dramatically altered the way the learner engaged in class as well.[20] Once learners felt that the adults were interested in who they were, their willingness to engage and contribute increased.

In BC, many schools have reported strong success in bringing a social and emotional pedagogy alive in the classroom through the Indigenous strategy of using a circle to start each day. After an invitational prompt, every learner's voice is heard and all learners are welcomed into the classroom community. This strategy applies to learners of all ages.

A few years ago, we were talking to a large group of rural teachers about the importance of the morning circle. At the prompting of one of her colleagues, one quiet teacher got to her feet to explain how she started the first class she saw every week with a circle check-in. She worked in a community where many families were struggling, and many learners had especially difficult times over the weekend. She said that she always made sure that the prompt for the check-in was positive. Then she sat down. After a moment of silence, her colleague stood up to fill in some more details.

He explained that there were students who never missed her class because of the chance to be heard. He also said that if on any day she decided to forego the check-in, her students refused to let her start the lesson until she did. Finally, he asked the crowd what grade they thought she taught. The assumption was that she was a primary teacher. He then explained that she taught senior chemistry and biology. Not only did her classes have almost perfect attendance but they also outperformed any other science class in the district. A simple strategy with a powerful impact.

In Queensland, we met a principal who was leading a complex elementary school. Drawing on the research about trauma-informed practice through the Berry Street model,[21] each class started the morning with an appreciative and personal check-in. They ended each day with a very short discussion of what they called WWW (What Went Well). Every day every student shared one learning highlight from the day. This simple act of starting and ending each day with every voice being heard created a deeper sense of identity and belonging.

We share these straightforward strategies as examples of what is working across a range of contexts. There are a great many resources for schools to consider if social-emotional learning has been selected as a focus. We encourage inquiry teams to take a close look at the available resources and then decide which best fits your context.[22] A number of schools are finding *The Social-Emotional Learning Toolbox* by Kathy Perez to be an especially useful resource. Whether your focus is conflict resolution, empathy, mindfulness, growth mindset, resilience, anxiety, or connectedness, take your time to explore the possibilities.

Once you have decided the best fit for your school, then gather the resources—whether in print, video, online, from a local consultant, from expertise already on staff, or from a school down the block or across the globe. Consider a virtual school tour.[23] Reach out to the knowledge base and dig into new professional learning.

ASSESSMENT FOR LEARNING

For the past two decades, we have been working with schools, districts, and networks to apply the research evidence on assessment for learning. Our interest in formative assessment was sparked by reading "Inside the Black Box: Raising Standards Through Classroom Assessment" (1998) by Paul Black and Dylan Wiliam. Our commitment to changing assessment practices to develop stronger and more confident learners continues to be a priority.

We believed that helping leaders develop the knowledge and skills to assist teachers to change their assessment practices (away from constant marking and scoring toward a greater emphasis on coaching for improvement) would have a positive impact on all learners. As a result, knowledge about assessment for learning became a central feature of the graduate leadership programs we were responsible for and the networks we lead.[24]

The timing of the publication of "Inside the Black Box" was particularly fortuitous for educators in BC. As we mentioned in our introduction, the funding provided by the Ministry of Education in 1999 was designed to encourage educators to access and then use the recently developed learning progressions in literacy, numeracy, and social responsibility. This was the start of NOIIE.

The original research published in "Inside the Black Box" led to global interest in assessment for learning, with numerous researchers and practitioners developing resources for use in schools. In 2015, Dylan Wiliam, this time in collaboration with Siobhán Leahy, followed up with *Embedding Formative Assessment: Practical Techniques for K–12 Classrooms*. By this point they had organized assessment for learning practice into five key strategies, which we quote here:

1. Clarifying, sharing and understanding learning intentions and success criteria
2. Engineering effective discussion, tasks, and activities that elicit evidence of learning
3. Providing feedback that moves learning forward
4. Activating students as learning resources for one another
5. Activating students as owners of their own learning[25]

Lorna Earl's subsequent contribution to the field in 2013 with *Assessment As Learning* helped to heighten the awareness of the importance of assessment as a game changer, especially for vulnerable learners. Katie White then published two books offering practical approaches to assessment for learning; these are striking a chord with many Canadian educators, as is Myron Dueck's 2021 book, *Giving Students a Say: Smarter Assessment Practices to Empower and Engage.*

On a study tour to New Zealand in 2015, we visited a school that provided an intensive professional program of support focused on assessment for learning over a six-year period.[26] Every teacher who joined this staff had a full year of coaching to develop their assessment repertoire. The school was humming with positive energy. The dedication to assessment for learning was evident in the student photos and statements posted around the school that communicated the commitment of the staff to families and learners. One statement said, "I am becoming a reflective learner who knows and acts on my strengths, achievements and next learning steps."

Learner agency

There is a strong connection between strengthening formative assessment and developing learner agency. Deborah L. Butler, Leyton Schnellert, and Nancy E. Perry's book *Developing Self-Regulating Learners* is a must-read resource for inquiry teams focused on increasing learner agency. It offers compelling evidence that "learners are empowered when they have opportunities to exercise *agency* in their lives and in their learning."[27] Students are demonstrating agency when they can explain in their own words what they are learning, why it is important, how they are doing it, and what their next steps will be.

Developing Self-Regulating Learners explains that there are two complementary aspects to an individual's experience of agency in a given activity. The first is strongly connected to their perceptions of self-efficacy: "When individuals believe in their personal capacities, they feel more empowered to achieve valued goals in real situations and activities. They are also more likely to take up activities, invest effort and persist through challenges."[28]

The second aspect of agency depends on learners' perception that they have a voice in the direction their lives are taking. The authors suggest a number of practices that support learners in having a meaningful voice in what and how they are learning. These include the following:

- Including students in co-constructing classroom norms, learning goals, and activities[29]
- Engaging students in activities that are "complex by design," especially those that include more open-ended, self-directed, or "experiential" forms of learning[30]
- Providing opportunities and supports for students to make productive, meaningful choices (e.g., topics, processes, how to represent learning)[31]

- Supporting students to learn how to take deliberate strategic control over learning across different kinds of activities and environments[32]
- Engaging students in ongoing, dynamic forms of peer and self-assessment[33]

Assessment for learning combined with an expeditionary spirit

Ron Berger, in his work with the Expeditionary Learning Network,[34] has made an exceptional contribution to whole-school change by drawing on his own experiences as an Outward Bound instructor,[35] an elementary teacher, and a skilled craftsman dedicated to creating beautiful woodwork.

Two books by this leader and his colleagues bring together the spirit of Outward Bound learning and powerful assessment practices: *Leaders of Their Own Learning: Transforming Schools Through Student-Engaged Assessment* and *The Leaders of Their Own Learning Companion: New Tools and Tips for Tackling the Common Challenges of Student-Engaged Assessment*. *Austin's Butterfly*,[36] a video Ron Berger created to demonstrate the use of models, criteria, and feedback with first-grade and kindergarten students, has been viewed by hundreds of thousands of educators, parents, and students around the globe. If you haven't seen this yet, it is a must. A third book, *We Are Crew*, is a valuable resource for educators who want to focus on building learner confidence and teamwork skills.

The Leaders of Their Own Learning Companion describes eight assessment dimensions that shift school practices to the place where young people truly do own their own learning:

1. Setting learning targets
2. Checking for understanding during daily lessons
3. Using evidence with learners
4. Using models, critiques, and descriptive feedback
5. Student-led conferences
6. Celebrations of learning
7. Passage presentations with portfolios
8. Standards-based grading[37]

The authors also caution that this work is not easy:

> The practices of student-engaged assessment cannot be plugged in and turned on. Using these practices well demands a growth mindset and the courage to take risks, a professional culture of collaboration and support, and a commitment to working together over time to customize these practices to work in your setting.[38]

As your inquiry team considers the focus for your professional learning, ask yourselves whether every teacher in your school is confident in their ability to provide coaching forms of feedback. Is every student able to say not only what they are learning and why it is important, but also how they are doing it and what their own next steps are to strengthen their learning in that specific domain or competency? As an inquiry team, are you willing to make the kind of commitment that is required to make this a reality?

The challenge of making assessment for learning a way of life requires a long-term commitment and ongoing professional learning. There is a direct link between learners' identity, sense of belonging, and well-being and the forms of assessment they experience.

Another key element in developing learner agency and intellectual engagement is connected to building curiosity in everyday learning activities. This takes us to a brief exploration of the power of inquiry at the classroom level.

INQUIRY-BASED LEARNING

In "Prospects and Challenges for Inquiry-Based Approaches to Learning," researchers Brigid Barron and Linda Darling-Hammond summarize some key understandings about how to do inquiry-based pedagogy well. They argue that students need to explore "real life situations and consequential problems" if they are to be well prepared for future challenges.[39] They also point out that to do this well requires a complex and sophisticated form of learning and teaching.

Australian educator Kath Murdoch has devoted her career to helping school communities reach higher levels of performance—and deeper levels of learning—through inquiry learning. Her book *The Power of Inquiry* is a very useful resource for leadership teams intent on developing more inquiry-based learning within classrooms and across the school. She explains that inquiry learning is an approach that demands higher-order thinking where students are continually challenged by the teacher, and tasks are designed for students to question, predict, gather, analyze, synthesize, and reflect.

The Power of Inquiry also insists that teachers need to understand the purpose of inquiry teaching and outlines many important reasons for investing in this pedagogical model. Well-constructed inquiry approaches contribute strongly to learner motivation. It is widely acknowledged that all of us are "more motivated to learn when we are genuinely interested in or curious about the subject, or when we have a problem we need to solve."[40]

This valuable resource for educators maintains that inquiry is another way to develop students' agency:

> Through quality questioning and involving students in actively gathering and analyzing information, the student gradually develops a sense of control over and responsibility for themselves as a learner. They learn to learn. Teachers nurture independence by gradually releasing responsibility and encouraging students to "make meaning" using high-level thinking skills and strategies.[41]

In learning sessions, on her blog, and in her book, Kath Murdoch outlines many important activities and strategies that strong inquiry teachers "do." Perhaps the most influential strategy is the final one she describes:

> The best inquiry teachers are *continually inquiring into their own practice*. They show students *they* are learners too—and bring an inquiry mindset to their own teaching. One of the most powerful ways we can nurture an inquiring disposition in our students is to show them our fascination in the world, our hunger to learn, our delight in discovery, our willingness to find out more and our preparedness to change our thinking. An inquiry mindset can be contagious when we make it visible and audible to others.[42]

A follow-up book by the same author, *Getting Personal With Inquiry Learning: A Practical Guide to Working With Young Learners' Questions, Passions, Interests and the Issues That Matter to Them*, makes the connection between personal inquiry and the need to belong:

> The need to belong is one of the most powerful drivers of human experience[,] and yet for many young people, schools are not environments in which they feel they belong. When we expect everyone to learn the same thing in the same way, we can marginalize so many. However, when we choose to respect and respond to the interests, curiosities, needs and passions of each learner, we can create a more inclusive environment. Personal inquiry offer[s] more scope to embrace what we now understand to be diverse cultural, gender and ethnic identities within our classroom communities and to better honour and champion neurodiversity over the traditional paradigm of conformity.[43]

An important additional feature of inquiry learning models is how well they complement nature- and place-based learning environments. *The Power of Inquiry* makes the personal connections with uncertainty and inquiry in nature in this way:

> I am often reminded of why I love inquiry teaching when I am lucky enough to find myself in nature with children. We all know that amazing moment when we are walking with children and we notice something extraordinary—perhaps we see it but they don't. So, we wait... we don't want to spoil the thrill of discovery. We may subtly guide them, help them move in the right direction and then suddenly—they see it. "Wow! Look at that!" And we delight in watching them discover something for themselves. In the same way, my inquiry mindset reminds me to remain open to new pathways. There are times when the route, or even the destination I have in mind, is changed. Intent on what I thought was the direction, I am persuaded to take another path.[44]

PLACE- AND NATURE-BASED LEARNING

In their book *Thrive: The Purpose of Schools in a Changing World*, Valerie Hannon and Amelia Peterson present a compelling case that "a fundamental learning goal will become learning how to live within the earth's renewable resources, protecting its ecosystems and biodiversity."[45] They acknowledge the contributions that diverse Indigenous communities bring to a broader understanding of how to live in relationship with nature. *Thrive* argues that "we can no longer conceive of the quality of human life without seeing ourselves as a part of nature."[46] This resource also draws on the work of Howard Gardner, who in 1995 revised his initial propositions about multiple intelligences by adding the concept of *naturalistic intelligence*, which is a holistic understanding of the world and its complexities.

Paul Clarke, the author of *Education for Sustainability: Becoming Naturally Smart*, believes that education is perfectly placed to create the conditions for all young people to become naturally smart. He suggests that the place to begin is to get outside in nature and connect with the environment that is immediately available. He encourages teachers to do this in simple stages by beginning in the schoolyard or under a tree, watching cloud formations or looking at the stars. He argues that by reconnecting learners to a sense of their own place, they will develop new insights about the importance of place that can ultimately lead to new solutions to existing challenges.

So what did Ann Marie and her colleagues learn and how did they go about it? They looked for resources that spoke to their need to understand the role of nature in helping their young learners develop a stronger sense of connection to place. Over the summer the staff agreed to read *Braiding Sweetgrass* by Robin Kimmerer. They found inspiration in the work of another school that had moved learning onto the land.[47] They explored the concept of a walking curriculum,[48] developed by Gillian Judson, a leader in Imaginative Ecological

Education, and they were especially pleased to discover a new resource—the website *Walking Forward, Learning from Place,* by Indigenous educator Heidi Wood and Gillian Judson. This resource illustrates the connections between a walking curriculum and the long history of Indigenous knowledge about learning on and from the land.

Ann Marie and her colleagues consulted with local Indigenous Elders, and they discovered that Jenny, one of the staff on their early childhood team, had Indigenous ancestry and a wealth of knowledge about Indigenous practices. She was eager to share her understandings. Jenny took the staff outside for walks and opened up their thinking about how to use the community garden and a local park as extensions to their classrooms. As a staff they read, they talked, they asked questions, they researched, they explored, they learned, and they grew.

Designing and supporting new professional learning around the identified needs of the learners you serve is a key responsibility of the leadership team. There is a lot to think about when designing professional learning. This chapter has focused primarily on ideas related to building connectedness through social-emotional learning, building stronger assessment practices to enhance learner agency, fostering curiosity through inquiry-based learning, and helping students develop a stronger connection to place. We can think of this as the *what* of professional learning. As leadership teams, you also need to consider the *how*; in other words, how you will design professional learning in a way that engages all adult learners and leads to an increase in professional capacity. This will be the focus of the next chapter.

A REMINDER ABOUT NEW PROFESSIONAL LEARNING:

New Professional Learning Is

- Directly linked to the focus identified in the earlier stages of the Spiral
- Motivated by, and connected to, changing the experiences of your learners
- Exploratory in testing how new approaches could be better than previous practices
- Tailored to your unique school setting

New Professional Learning Is Not

- Pursuing the latest trends
- Uncritically adopting new ways without understanding the purpose
- Only for a short-term or quick fix
- Disconnected from your context

BIG IDEAS FROM CHAPTER 5

- New professional learning is directly linked to the focus for your inquiry.
- An understanding of the why (theory) and the how (practice) of new learning is required for lasting changes in practice.
- Professional learning involves the consideration of wise, strong, and new ways.
- Developing student sense of belonging and agency is directly linked to motivation and engagement.
- A sense of belonging is directly related to well-being and the capacity to thrive in uncertain times.
- Formative assessment is key.

FREQUENTLY ASKED QUESTIONS ABOUT NEW LEARNING

There are so many resources out there. How will we know if we are selecting the best one?

Whether you are choosing a book, a video series, a set of articles, or a consultant to work with your team, make sure that you can draw a direct link between the resource, the identified needs of your learners, and the focus you have selected. Drawing on external expertise from your local university or colleagues in another school with a similar focus can help you make better decisions. Applying the decision framework at this stage in the Spiral can also be helpful. Involve the team in exploring the various resources and come to a consensus as a group as to which approach—or approaches—best suits your school.

There is so much for us to learn from Indigenous perspectives. How do we get started?

Many teachers who have not had the opportunity to learn much about the Indigenous roots of their place, whether in Canada, the USA, Australia, or any other colonized country, are often concerned about making a mistake. We have experienced the incredible generosity offered by Indigenous colleagues and community members when we have asked questions with a good heart and an open mind. We have been reassured that mistakes are part of learning. Within Canada there are many resources designed to help teachers get started. For example, Strong Nations is an Indigenous-owned online book and gift store as well as a publishing house that provides authentic resources for K–12 educators.[49] Our advice, regardless of where you live, is to check out local resources, read not only about the history but also about the current contributions of the Indigenous communities in your area, learn more about the territory you are inhabiting, and listen with respect to Indigenous colleagues and Elders.

QUESTIONS FOR LEARNING CONVERSATIONS

1. One of the First Peoples Principles of Learning is "Learning takes patience and time." How does this connect to your experience as a learner? How does it reflect your own experience so far with the Spiral of Inquiry?
2. Think about the most powerful professional learning you have experienced. What made this learning so valuable for you?
3. What is working right now in your school to develop a sense of belonging and connection? What resources did you draw on to create this culture of belonging? What more do you think you could do?
4. To what extent is assessment for learning a way of life across all learning settings in your school? If this is a major strength in your school, how did you get there? If there is more work to be done, how might you start?
5. How can you design more of the learning in your program to take place outdoors?

LEADERSHIP MOVES

- Make sure you don't skip this stage in your (or your team's) enthusiasm to move to action.
- Model new learning yourself. Search out and share resources that are connected to the focus for your inquiry and leave space for others to find resources.
- Don't make assumptions about your learners and their learning. Keep coming back to the key Spiral questions: "What's going on for our learners?" "How do we know?" Be persistently curious.

6

NEW PROFESSIONAL LEARNING

Designing for Change

Jasmine and Elaine are principals of secondary schools in a mid-sized Canadian district. Both their school teams had been involved in Spirals work for a year with a common focus on developing a greater sense of belonging for every learner—and especially for their Indigenous learners. Both school inquiry teams had been meeting occasionally to share ideas and compare notes. They had drawn on the wisdom of local Elders, and they had been studying ways to incorporate more Indigenous understandings across the curriculum. Small teams of teachers were taking on individual inquiries to increase learner agency and voice. Jasmine and Elaine wanted to build on the work that was starting to take hold and provide ways for other teachers to get involved.

They also wanted to do whatever they could to create the conditions for adult learning and curiosity. They designed a series of learning opportunities for the teams from both schools to dig deeper into their inquiries and to push each other's thinking. As they asked themselves what they could do to encourage more teachers from other schools to get involved, the idea of a curiosity cab emerged. Jasmine and Elaine wanted to build a resource for professional learning that was portable and that was also fun, engaging, relevant, and visual. In the first year, they loaded everyone on a bus, named it the curiosity cab, and moved participants from school to school. Once the pandemic hit, the cab became virtual as participants moved across schools on Zoom. They thought of a curiosity cab both as a real vehicle and also as a metaphor that creates a space for professional learning to be on the move.

If we are to make the kinds of changes that are required for every learner to cross the stage with dignity, purpose, and options, then as leaders we need to ensure that professional learning is at the core of what we do. How your inquiry team will make professional learning a key priority will vary depending on your unique context. What is non-negotiable, however, is the commitment to continuous learning that is modelled by every member of the team. Teachers, principals, and support staff, as well as young learners, must be able to respond on an ongoing basis to three key questions: "What am I learning and why is it important?" "How is it going?" and "What are my next steps?"

Helen Timperley's synthesis of current research on teacher professional learning underscores the critical importance of linking teacher learning to student needs. Her work also emphasizes the need for worthwhile content, for integration of knowledge and skills, and for the opportunity for teachers to learn in environments with high degrees of both trust and challenge.

In chapter 5 we introduced some ideas and resources that we think are worth considering at the New Professional Learning stage of the Spiral. This chapter will take you deeper into the New Professional Learning stage, as we will explore some key research findings about high-impact teacher professional learning. We will introduce the concept of symmetry in designing deeper learning and provide some questions for determining the current status of professional inquiry in your school. We will explore the ways in which adaptive expertise is developed through collaborative inquiry, and we will invite you to consider the importance of understanding the emotions involved in educational change. Finally, we will ask you to think about the stages of adult development and the implications for your professional learning designs.

TEACHER PROFESSIONAL LEARNING—GLOBAL INSIGHTS

Learning First, a research team led by Ben Jensen and based in Melbourne, Australia, conducted a study to examine what professional learning looked like in four high-performing systems—British Columbia (BC), Hong Kong, Shanghai, and Singapore. These systems were identified as high-performing based on a wide range of international measures. As long-time BC educators, we were pleased that our province was identified as a case for this study.

The starting point for these researchers' 2016 report was a review of effective professional learning and successful approaches to school change. This was followed by site visits and in-depth interviews with teachers, principals, district leaders, and policy-makers. Despite the significant cultural differences between BC and the Asian jurisdictions, the team identified five characteristics that were evident in each one of these systems:

- **Professional learning is inquiry-based.** Effective adult learning involves teachers pursuing important questions related to student learning.
- **Professional learning is collaborative.** The most powerful professional learning involves teams of teachers, support staff, and principals working together within and across schools.
- **Professional learning is linked and coherent.** Connecting teacher learning with identified student learning needs is key to developing a coherent approach. There may be a range of opportunities provided, but the strongest programs are linked to a common theme.
- **Professional learning is led by the profession.** Developing internal capacity while also drawing on external expertise—subject specialists, helping teachers, master teachers, inquiry coaches—was a key feature in each of the high-performing systems.

- **Professional learning takes place over time.** In the best systems, time for professional learning is built into the weekly routines of the school. Stand-alone workshops or one-shot events are the exception, not the norm.

We encourage you to think about the current designs for professional learning in your schools and districts. To what extent do these characteristics reflect your context? What are the strengths of your current approaches? Consider what you think needs to be changed to make professional learning even more powerful.

SYMMETRY AND DEEPER LEARNING

By engaging with the Spiral of Inquiry you are committing to creating more powerful learning experiences for the young people you serve. Recent research on deeper forms of learning takes us to the concept of symmetry and its relevance to adult learning designs.

Across the globe many secondary educators are concerned about low levels of student engagement. There is genuine interest in changing high-school experiences. Over a six-year period, Harvard researchers Jal Mehta and Sarah Fine took on an ambitious agenda as they went in search of exemplary teaching and learning practices in American secondary schools. Specifically, they were looking for deeper learning practices—ones that combined "the cognitive and the affective, the short-term and the long-term, and the individual and the social."[1]

To shape their work, they drew on the studies of individuals who had become especially knowledgeable in their area of interest. They identified a pattern that started with the learner initially playing around with a concept, a skill, or a tool. As these learners engaged in deliberate practice with a coach, they began to develop their skills. Eventually, as they reached mastery, they were able to be more playful and more creative in their area of interest. In their report, *In Search of Deeper Learning,* the researchers observe, "We could think of this process as a kind of spiral, in which one returns again and again to the same activities, but each time in a way that is more sophisticated."[2]

These researchers experienced challenges in finding whole schools or systems where deeper learning was a way of life. They did, however, find one small network of schools that was making real progress with project-based learning. Their analysis of the success of this network revealed three key factors:

1. **"Say no."** They noted the willingness of these schools to say no to unaligned goals and priorities in order to maintain the necessary coherence, alignment, and collective identity.
2. **Be visible.** They saw that standards for good work were highly visible and laced through many of their processes.
3. **Create symmetry.** They realized there was a symmetry between how the adults who worked in the school were socialized and developed and how they expected teachers to teach students.[3]

These findings have a direct connection to your work in designing adult learning in elementary, middle, and secondary schools. First, ensuring coherence by sticking with a worthwhile focus area over time (and by minimizing distractions) will lead to deeper adult learning. Second, adult learning should be visible. School goals, the focus for adult learning, and the ways in which adults are engaging in new learning need to be readily apparent throughout the school. What stories do the walls tell? What stories are communicated on the website, on Twitter, in school blogs, and through direct communication with families? Third, it makes sense that if we want to develop young people as critical thinkers and problem solvers, then educators must also develop these skills.

In Search of Deeper Learning explains what was expected for teachers in the schools where deeper learning was evident:

> Like students, teachers are expected to draw on their divergent experiences and passions, blurring the boundaries between who they are outside and inside of school in service of creating divergent work. Like students, teachers must learn to collaborate productively and to manage collaboration-based conflicts as they arise. Like students, teachers learn through the process of iteratively revising their plans and "failing forward." Like students, teachers are afforded a large measure of autonomy that is framed by ongoing support and an overall culture of transparency. Finally, like students, teachers are treated as creative agents deserving of trust and respect.[4]

This research on schools that are creating more engaging and deeper forms of learning highlights some important considerations for adult professional learning. Coherence, visibility, trust, respect, collaboration, and support are key features at every stage of the Spiral and are especially critical at the New Professional Learning stage.

Schools as learning organizations

For the last several years, a growing number of scholars and policy-makers have called for reconceptualizing schools as learning organizations. This concept, although well received, has lacked clarity until recently. Marco Kools and Louise Stoll have made a significant contribution to this discussion. They identify seven dimensions that are associated with schools that function as strong learning organizations. These are:

- Shared vision developed through partnerships
- Continuous professional learning
- Team collaboration
- Inquiry and innovation culture
- Systems for knowledge exchange
- Environmental learning
- Learning leadership[5]

Many jurisdictions are finding this framework very helpful in their overall planning for system change. Fortunately, these researchers have developed a series of survey questions that schools can use to help determine the current strengths and areas of challenge connected to each of the seven dimensions.

We encourage inquiry teams to take a close look at the fourth dimension, which has to do with building a culture of inquiry and curiosity. Understanding where your school is at with regard to an inquiry culture can help you identify specific areas that require attention as you design new professional learning. The following questions can serve as prompts for your team. You might consider choosing four or five of these aspects of a culture of curiosity to explore with your staff:

To what extent would you agree that:

- Staff have opportunities to experiment with and practice new skills
- Staff are encouraged to take initiative
- Staff are supported when taking calculated risks
- Staff spend time exploring a problem before taking action
- Staff engage in inquiry (i.e., pose questions, gather and use evidence to decide how to change their practice and evaluate its impact)
- Staff are open to thinking and doing things differently
- Staff are open to others questioning their beliefs, opinions and ideas
- Staff openly discuss failures in order to learn from them
- Problems are seen as opportunities for learning[6]

As your team engages in the Spiral of Inquiry, not only are you working to change the experiences of your learners in substantive ways but you are also creating a culture of professional curiosity and inquiry across the school. Knowing your starting point as a staff can help you determine the extent to which you are moving your school toward being a true learning organization.

DEVELOPING ADAPTIVE EXPERTISE

Here are two claims for you to consider: First, complex problems require adaptive expertise. Second, adaptive expertise is developed through collaborative inquiry.

As mentioned previously, the Spiral of Inquiry is designed to address complex learning challenges for which the solutions are not readily apparent. Most significant learning challenges require new learning, experimentation, discoveries, and changes to established practices. This takes us to the concept of adaptive expertise and how it is developed through collaborative inquiry.

Important ideas about adaptive expertise were first proposed by in 1986 by Giyoo Hatano and Kayoko Inagaki. These two Japanese scholars suggest a way of connecting levels of innovation with levels of efficiency. This work was intriguing to Deirdre Le Fevre and her colleagues at the University of Auckland, who then applied these ideas to adult professional learning. In *Leading Powerful Professional Learning*, these researchers suggest the following distinctions:

> Practitioners who were highly efficient but did not innovate much were described as *routine experts*. Practitioners who innovated a lot but were not very efficient were described as *frustrated novices*. Practitioners who were highly innovative and also efficient were described as *adaptive experts*. Adaptive experts were able to flex to changing circumstances with insight and efficiency.[7]

As leadership teams strive to address complex problems related to student learning, understanding the differences between routine and adaptive expertise is helpful. Here is a brief framework for making these distinctions:

ROUTINE	ADAPTIVE
Applies a set of skills with increasing fluency and efficiency	Flexibly retrieves, organizes, and applies professional knowledge
Takes own beliefs for granted, is not open to scrutiny	Understands that own beliefs underpin practice, acknowledges when they get in the way
Seeks to progress from novice to expert, believes "practice makes perfect"	Recognizes when old problems persist or new problems arise and seeks expert knowledge

Educational expertise depends on context. A teacher might demonstrate adaptive expertise in one situation but not in another. Given the complexity of student needs, it is important to be able to move in and out of using routine and adaptive expertise almost seamlessly depending on the problem or the complexity of the situation.

A common mistake in education is to think that problems are simple when in reality they may be quite complex. A strategy that works effectively in one setting may be a major disappointment in another. *Leading Powerful Professional Learning* suggests that there are some signs that indicate that a problem (originally considered simple) is actually complex. For example, interventions have been tried but the results are disappointing. Teachers have experienced a lot of workshops in a key area and are able to "talk the talk," but very few new strategies are evident in classroom observations. No one can really explain why.

Most educational problems are complex because they involve people and processes. Even seemingly simple routines, such as designing morning meetings or developing a school-wide math assessment, can end up being quite complex. The challenge for inquiry teams is to understand how people are responding to the proposed changes and how to ensure the new learning is relevant to real problems of practice. Your leadership team has to be ready to challenge assumptions in ways that stimulate curiosity and reflection while reducing anger and defensiveness.

Intentional interruption is key. Many of us tend to engage in the world in ways that confirm what we already know or believe. Schools are such busy places that often teachers do not have enough time to think deeply on a regular basis. Adaptive expertise, however, develops in cultures that intentionally engage people in learning, problem-solving, and disruption of assumptions.

The schools that we work with vary significantly in the amount of time and resources available for professional learning. Regardless of the amount of available financial resources, however, creative leadership teams find ways to provide time during the school day for teachers to engage in the kind of dialogue that builds adaptive expertise. Even a half hour of dedicated time each week can make a difference.

In a presentation at the 2019 Networks of Inquiry and Indigenous Education symposium,[8] Helen Timperley shared the following graphic to help participants understand the connection between complicated and complex problems and the link with the Spiral of Inquiry.

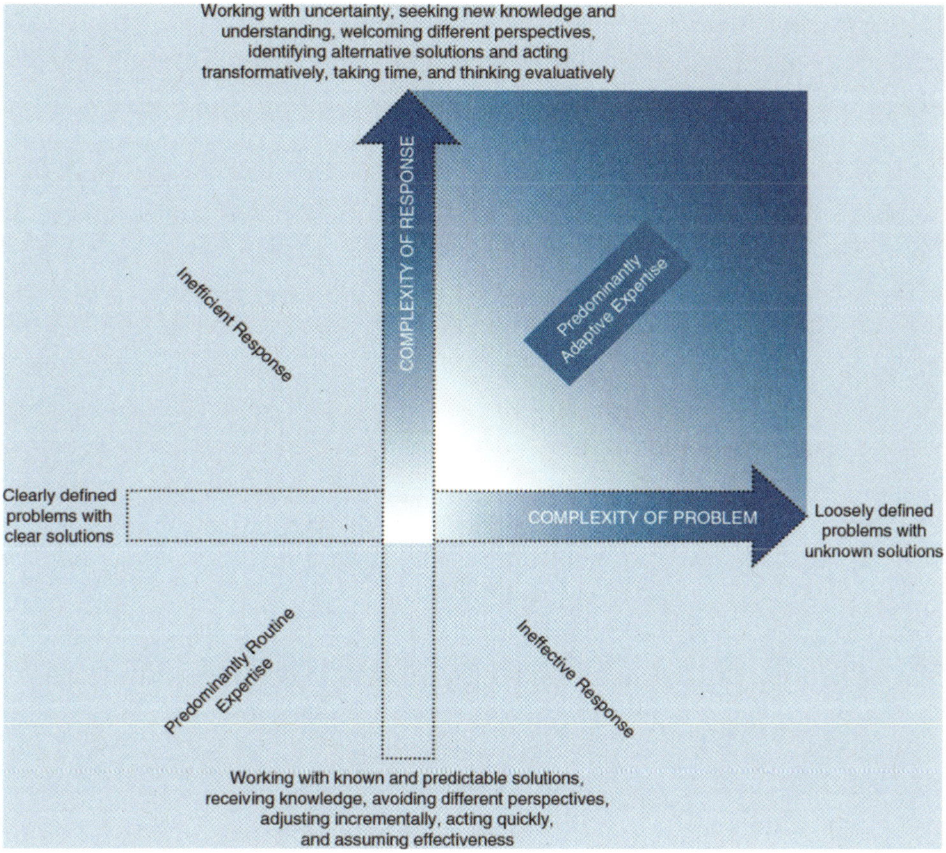

Figure 6.1. Routine and Adaptive Expertise

Deirdre M. Le Fevre, Helen Timperley, Kaye Twyford, and Fiona Ell, *Leading Powerful Professional Learning: Responding to Complexity With Adaptive Expertise* (Corwin Press, 2020), p. 124. Courtesy of Corwin Press.

The more complex the problem is, the more complex the response needs to be. Over time, teachers as adaptive experts are able to respond both effectively and efficiently to new challenges.

LEARNING FROM OTHER SCHOOLS

Sometimes the richest resources for new professional learning are not found in books, in videos, or on websites but within the walls of a school just down the street—or perhaps somewhere across the world. Over the past several years we have had the opportunity to host formal study tours from England, Sweden, Spain, Germany, Australia, Switzerland, and Aotearoa/New Zealand as well as visitors from the US. In every case we learned a great deal from seeing BC schools through the eyes of informed and appreciative visitors.

Study tours have not been a part of the BC culture to the same extent as in some other countries. We realized that this kind of opportunity was not a way of life for BC teachers and that many teachers and principals hadn't visited schools in the same district, let alone schools in other parts of the world. We wanted more educators to have the same kind of experience that is reflected in these comments from Christopher Martin, a school leader in Sydney, Australia, after visiting BC schools:

> I was truly inspired by the way storytelling holds such a vital place in pedagogy. There were examples all around us, in so many schools, of the personal stories of each child being shared and celebrated—their families, their culture, their heritage, their language. The power of stories and the notion of finding stories all around us—in nature, in loose parts, in art and in shared and personal histories—was so tangible and has motivated change, not just in my classroom but across my school.[9]

So we invited Catherine Ludwig, a network leader and school principal, to develop a guide for school study tours based on her experience as a principal hosting various groups. The resulting *Learning Tour Study Guide*, which is available for free online, provides a helpful outline for school tours—both virtual and in person—where the focus is on curiosity about inquiry frameworks. The study guide includes tips for engaging, questions to consider, and points to resources inquiry teams might find helpful. This guides educators to:

- **Learn from the struggles** as well as the successes and work in progress. You will be better prepared to take risks when you understand the potential pitfalls. Inquiry is iterative: every school will be a work in progress. Look for evidence of the path they are taking.

- **Step outside your comfort zone.** Visiting schools that do not look or feel anything like where you come from can help you to envision new possibilities and consider your work in new ways.
- **Probe for learning, not teaching.** Remember it is not only "teaching" that causes learning. Look and listen for how students engage and interact in their environment. What conditions are in place to make this space safe for learning?[10]

The guide provides a four-part framework to help organize the tour:

1. **Open**—What are you hoping to learn from the tour?[11]
2. **Observe**—What evidence of learning do you observe in each setting?[12]
3. **Ask**—What do you wonder? Ask focused but open-ended questions.[13]
4. **Receive**—What resonates? ... Reflect on the stories people share.[14]

This guide takes school teams well beyond an educational tourism experience to one where new learning can really take hold. We encourage inquiry teams to consider the learning opportunities that a visit to another school might provide and to use the suggestions in the study guide to maximize the impact of their visit.

LIVING WITH SOME UNCERTAINTY

At this point in the Spiral, as a leadership team, you have identified a complex focus for your inquiry—one that involves new learning and requires people to change. Developing adaptive expertise requires being able to live with a certain degree of discomfort; this takes acceptance that not knowing is part of the process. In chapter 5, we introduced you to the notion of *Cwelelep*, a learning principle from the Líl̓wat people. This means recognizing the need to sometimes be "in a place of dissonance [and] uncertainty"[15] so as to be open to new learning. An inquiry culture accepts that uncertainty is a normal part of the process of learning more deeply.

In *Leading Professional Learning*, Helen Timperley, Fiona Ell, Deirdre Le Fevre, and Kaye Twyford point out the following:

> Prior to engagement in an inquiry process, it is difficult to describe exactly what is expected because it is not a prescriptive process. However, as teachers become more familiar with the process and the changes expected, their perceptions of risk decrease.[16]

At each stage in the Spiral, we encourage you to keep student learning at the centre by regularly asking, "What's going on for our learners? How do we know? And why does it matter?" These questions can help move teams toward adaptive expertise by continuously challenging assumptions that may have become hard-wired in routines.

We also recognize that educators can feel highly vulnerable when their assumptions and routines are challenged. Change is easy to talk about. It's much harder to realize. Feelings of risk and vulnerability, feelings of fear and uncertainty, and perceptions of risk are social-emotional aspects of professional learning that must be addressed if you are to get the improved outcomes for your learners that are needed.

EMOTION, RISK, AND UNCERTAINTY IN TEACHER PROFESSIONAL LEARNING

Significant changes in learning and teaching practices can provide real challenges to teacher identity and confidence. There is evidence that indicates that those leadership teams that consider ways to reduce feelings of vulnerability make the best progress with engaging teachers in new learning. A curious and empathetic stance is much more useful than one in which colleagues are described as "resistant."

Helen Timperley, Fiona Ell, Deirdre Le Fevre, and Kaye Twyford's findings about teacher attitudes to professional learning and risk-taking are particularly relevant to leadership teams at this point in the Spiral. They point out that teaching is full of uncertainty: "Nothing seems good enough anymore, with constant questions being asked about the meaning of progress, the ways to achieve it and the difficulties of knowing what has been achieved."[17]

When faced with these complex circumstances, teachers are often in a heightened emotional state. Facing new challenges often increases perceptions of risk. This in turn creates feelings of vulnerability, especially for those who have had negative experiences with past forms of professional learning. The authors of *Leading Professional Learning* maintain that risk in this context is not about danger—it's all about uncertainty. Teachers ask themselves, "What is expected of me? Will I have to change? Will I be able to? Do I want to?"[18]

Effective inquiry leadership teams recognize the individual needs and emotions of the participants. They understand that teachers are more likely to take the risks necessary to learn new approaches when they feel secure in their relationships with their colleagues and when they respect those leading the sessions. In the past, emotion in our profession was often seen as a weakness or a problem. New teachers were sometimes encouraged "to leave their feelings at the door." What an unfortunate and potentially harmful message to convey. It's now clear that emotion, cognition, and motivation work together in complex, inseparable ways.

Formal leaders who are often highly action-oriented must remind themselves of the emotional needs of their teachers. Not every teacher is willing to leap into new forms of action. Some teachers find change intimidating and risky. Risk can't be totally eliminated because of the complex nature of the learning and teaching environment. Uncertainty can, nevertheless, be reduced. Wise inquiry leadership teams strive to get the balance right by encouraging enough risk so that changes can get underway without creating so much uncertainty that teachers feel afraid to try. Feelings of risk and uncertainty can be reduced with a clearly articulated purpose, well-organized learning sessions that acknowledge emotions, a supportive environment, and frequent checking in throughout the Spiral process.

It's important for the leaders of the inquiry process—whether formal or informal —to express their own emotions and feelings of vulnerability:

> Making public what you experience as a leader acknowledges that emotion is an inevitable part of learning and change and is sometimes uncomfortable or even distressing. Providing teachers with structured opportunities to do the same can open up conversations and potentially identify commonalities between the concerns of leaders and those of teachers.[19]

Public learning and a focus on an individual learner

An effective approach that we have seen work in a range of different situations involves teachers and inquiry teams focusing on one individual learner as a way to open up thinking about potential new approaches. Lead by Learning (formerly

Mills Scholars) is a network of schools and districts in California that all share an interest in developing professional curiosity and increasing equity for their learners.[20] For over a decade, Carrie Wilson has been working with this organization, helping to develop and use strategies that amplify teacher agency. She describes this work in "Making Learning Public: Valuing Teachers' Voices," a chapter in Shane Safir and Jamila Dugan's book *Street Data*.

In this chapter we learn about the fishbowl style of public learning. A group of educators observe two teachers describe a learning challenge they are currently working through. This conversation often involves the discussion of a focal student. "This is a practice that allows teachers to see individual learners and their individual approaches to learning. It supports a deep dive, an asset-based stance, an opportunity to ground abstract goals in a student's lived experience."[21]

Changing Results for Young Readers was a major early literacy initiative in BC from 2012–15 that was followed by Changing Results for Young Children[22]—with a focus on early learning more generally. In each of these initiatives, teachers were asked to apply the Spiral of Inquiry and to focus on one student, usually described as a *wonder learner*. A wonder learner is the kind of learner that teachers struggle to figure out. The teacher might wonder, for example, "What is blocking this child's understanding of reading?" Or, "What is preventing their enjoyment of reading?" Concentrating on one specific learner, rather than on the whole class, helps teachers focus their efforts. The underlying premise is that as teachers adapt their teaching for that one child, they will learn a great deal that will benefit many others in their class.

PROFESSIONAL LEARNING AND ADULT STAGES OF DEVELOPMENT

In addition to appreciating the challenges of developing adaptive expertise; addressing risk, emotion, and uncertainty; and modelling vulnerability, inquiry teams we know have found the research on the stages of adult development helpful and practical. This area of study comes from the work of Robert Kegan, a Harvard psychologist. Eleanor Drago-Severson, a professor of educational leadership and adult learning and leadership at Teachers College, Columbia University, has worked intensively to apply his findings to K–12 education.

Ways of knowing

In *Leading Change Together: Developing Educator Capacity Within Schools and Systems*, Eleanor Drago-Severson and Jessica Blum-DeStefano point out that knowledge about adult stages of development can help create stronger and more transformational programs of professional learning for teachers and support staff. They outline four different "ways of knowing in adulthood—instrumental, socializing, self-authoring, and self-transforming"—and they explain why these matter for leadership teams.[23] According to these researchers, an adult's way of knowing or meaning-making system is "the lens through which all of life's experiences are filtered."[24]

The **instrumental way of knowing** is based on the conviction that there are right and wrong ways to do things. The firmly held belief that one particular way is "right" and that the "rules" suggest only one approach is connected with a stance that asks, "How can I get the things I want and need? What is in this approach for me?"[25] Many teachers in the first few years of their career have this way of knowing. They value routines and strategies that help them manage the complexity of their learning environments. They appreciate concrete ideas that work.

The **socializing way of knowing** is framed by a view that "What you think of me and my teaching/learning practices is what I think of me."[26] Staff members who have this way of knowing are influenced by the "values, beliefs, feelings, and perspectives of people whom they care about and respect."[27] They connect with emotions and feel responsible for the feelings of others. They want to fit in and will usually support the direction of the group, whether they are firmly committed to it or not.

The **self-authoring way of knowing** asks, "Am I living, working, and loving up to my full potential? Am I demonstrating my competencies at home, at work, and in life?"[28] Adults at this stage of development find it easy to understand the points of view of other people. At the same time, they are very concerned with meeting their own internal standards based on values and competencies. They are self-directed and independent thinkers.

The **self-transforming way of knowing** asks, "How can we learn from and with each other to grow different parts of ourselves?"[29] Educators in this stage of development can take a stand based on their principles, but they are also very open to the beliefs and values of others. They actively work to understand perspectives that they do not hold themselves in order to build connections with a broader range of people. They are bridge-builders. This is the rarest of the developmental stages.

In every school it is likely that there will be staff members at each one of the stages. It is also possible that people are at different stages depending on the situation. This has implications for inquiry leadership teams, especially for those involved in shifting schools from transmission-learning models to transformational-learning models with the goal of achieving deeper learning.

In *Leading Change Together* we learn:

> Transformational learning has to do with increases in our cognitive, affective, interpersonal, and/or intrapersonal capacities that enable us to manage better the complexities of learning, leading, teaching, and living. For example, we experience transformational learning when we begin to understand more about how others think and feel, when we intuit and appreciate others' perspectives, when we recognize and overcome worries that may previously have held us back (e.g. fear of conflict or of sharing our real thinking and feeling), when we turn toward difficult conversations and engage in them instead of avoiding them, or when we grow the capacity to see beyond our current constructions of how the world works.[30]

How this looks in practice

One secondary leadership team that we observed was determined to deepen staff knowledge and practice in formative assessment. Previous workshops had taken place, but there was little evidence of change in most classrooms.

The team thought hard about how they would use the precious hour and a half of learning time they had available at their next staff session. They wanted the meeting to build interest for ongoing work. They wanted to have a positive impact on teachers, with the ultimate goal that students who had been accustomed primarily to summative assessment would develop greater agency as learners. The team also wanted to respect the various worldviews held by their colleagues.

They decided to first focus on the importance of clear learning intentions as a high leverage strategy. Several of the team leaders had visited a school serving a similar demographic—one that had made assessment for learning a school-wide way of life. They acquired some new insights from this experience, and they had a better idea of what formative assessment practices looked like in a range of content areas.

Their intentions for this first staff session were to build knowledge, have teachers practise developing a clear learning intention to try out in the following week, and have educators leave the session feeling confident in the overall direction of the professional learning work. They were aware that they were working with adult learners who would all understand and see things in different ways.

A thoughtfully designed and carefully considered program of professional learning has the potential to enable staff to understand more, to see more, and to deal with complexities of learning and teaching in more sophisticated ways. To address the needs of adults at different stages of development, this team did the following during this first session:

- They included a part of the meeting where they provided strong concrete examples of the big ideas connected to an important aspect of the new curriculum. (Instrumental knowers, and many teachers new to the profession, do best with concrete examples and clear directions.)
- They acknowledged strong practices seen during walkthroughs and talks with students and by observing what was featured on bulletin boards and in communication with families. (Socializing knowers appreciate positive mention of things that are going well.)
- They provided a section where individuals could set their own goals and decide on their own course of action. (Self-authoring educators like to be recognized for their competence and expertise, and they enjoy making their own decisions.)
- They built in time for the participants to engage in team conversations and to hear various points of view. (Self-transforming educators like to stretch their own thinking by hearing the views of others and building meaningful connections with them.)

The inquiry leadership team was pleased and relieved when this introductory meeting went well. Although the success of this meeting wasn't completely tied to their consideration of stages of development, they thought it had helped. Teachers paired up and made a commitment to each other for the actions they were prepared to make, and they agreed to check for understanding with their learners. They expressed genuine interest in sharing what they had learned at their next formal meeting.

When Jasmine and Elaine came up with the idea of the learning series and the curiosity cab, they weren't entirely sure what they were getting into. They asked a few colleagues for advice, and they reached out to members of their own staffs for suggestions and feedback. They modelled transparency, teamwork, and vulnerability. They shared a lot of laughs and their own apprehensions. They demonstrated to their colleagues that they were willing to try something entirely new without any guarantee that it would work perfectly the first time.

And how did Elaine and Jasmine build these understandings into the virtual curiosity cab? The curiosity cab came at the end of the year. School teams had participated in a set of three highly organized, interactive virtual sessions throughout the year focused on different stages of the Spiral. Each session included strategies for visible learning, sharing of resources, time to reflect on what had been done, and time to plan next steps.

The curiosity cab was a highly enjoyable online event that:

- kicked off with a playlist of Indigenous music
- included a learning-focused book giveaway
- used the Open, Observe, Ask, and Receive framework from the *Learning Tour Study Guide*

- **had focused five-minute videos from each of the four presenting schools**
- **provided time for comments and observations from everyone in the cab.**

The presenting teams were affirmed for their work and challenged to consider their next steps. Teachers left with new strategies, stronger connections, new insights, and a greater sense of community. Indigenous understandings were deepened. Not only was there great new learning but it was also a lot of fun. And this was all done in ninety minutes one day after school.

There is a lot to consider when designing adult learning. Leadership teams need to appreciate that staff members are at different stages of adult development and make sure their plans address the needs of staff at each of these four stages. The goals and purposes of adult learning need to be communicated clearly and made visible to the entire school community. Professional learning must be well-organized, coherent, and linked to the overall focus for change. Educators must be supported in developing new expertise and encouraged to question routine practices that may or may not be working as intended. Creating the conditions where feelings of vulnerability are acknowledged and welcomed can build trust and help develop a learning culture.

All of this work takes patience and time. By applying the knowledge of teacher professional learning to this stage of the Spiral we can increase the chances that new learning will lead to significant changes in practice and that these in turn will have a positive impact on the experiences of learners.

BIG IDEAS FROM CHAPTER 6

- Professional learning in strong systems is inquiry-based, collaborative, led by the profession, linked and coherent, and takes place over time.
- Symmetry in professional learning means that there is a direct link between the ways teachers learn and the way they are expected to teach.
- Adaptive expertise develops through collaborative inquiry and is required to address complex challenges for which there are no set answers.
- Emotions, risk, vulnerability, and uncertainty are all part of the change process.
- Educators may be at different stages of adult development, and this has implications for designing new learning.

FREQUENTLY ASKED QUESTIONS ABOUT NEW LEARNING

What do we do with people who aren't interested in changing?

This is probably the question we get asked most often. You may have asked it yourself and heard an answer like "Go with the goers" or received advice about how to encourage the reluctant to move on, perhaps to a different school. Ignoring those who are reluctant is disrespectful. Shuffling a so-called problem to another school is unprofessional. Our stance is that everyone wants to feel competent and good about their work. Sometimes the experiences individuals have had or their current situation, personally or professionally, have led them to build a defensive armour.

Building trust takes time and a lot of listening. Our very short answer is not to give up on anyone until you have exhausted every bit of listening energy. Acknowledge fear and uncertainty. Be direct and clear about the vision for change. Come back repeatedly to the voices of learners and their experiences as the motivation for the new direction. Don't make anyone feel guilt or shame about their unwillingness to jump in right away. Provide as much support as you can for those who are on the move. Always find a way for people to engage when they are ready.

Our district (state, province, authority) is mandating new learning in areas that are not entirely consistent with our values or our focus area. How do we make sure that our professional learning is linked and coherent?

It isn't easy to take a stand that, although right for your school, goes against the direction of your jurisdiction. Providing solid evidence from a thorough scan and a strong rationale for the focus you have selected may help in some situations. Sharing your own understanding about what makes powerful professional learning may be useful. Sometimes rocking the boat a little is just what is needed; in some contexts this may not be such a good idea. We have found that forming and sustaining a network helps to change policies and systems over time.

What is always within your sphere of influence is how you invest your time and energy. It may be that you have to, as the saying goes, "bow down to power" enough so that you don't jeopardize your position while at the same time taking advantage of every possible opportunity within the school to keep the focus on what matters most to your learners. Be intentional about every conversation and every interaction. Avoid getting sidetracked into blame or frustration. Put your energy into changing the experiences of your learners. Use the power of story to convey the changes that are underway.

QUESTIONS FOR LEARNING CONVERSATIONS

1. To what extent does your school have a culture of trust in which teachers are encouraged to try new approaches and to "fail forward"? As a leadership team, how will you make risk-taking feel less risky?
2. One way to maintain coherence is to say no to unaligned goals and priorities. What are your thoughts about how to do this in a way that is respectful of conflicting demands?
3. Intentional interruption and challenging of assumptions are necessary to build adaptive expertise. Generate some ideas about how you will do this in a way that maintains dignity and respect.

4. There is strong evidence from the research on trust in schools that trust is built when the leader— formal or informal—expresses vulnerability first. What do you think of this idea? What is your experience with vulnerability—as a teacher and as a leader?

5. Think about the next professional learning opportunity at your school. How will you design the session to address the needs of individuals reflecting different ways of knowing?

LEADERSHIP MOVES

- Make sure that the focus for adult professional learning is visible to your students, their parents, and your community.
- Do whatever you can to provide time during the day for professional learning. Be an active participant.
- Be intentional in designing professional learning— reduce risk, attend to the different stages of adult development, make sure all meetings are productive and well organized.
- As much as possible, say no to initiatives or demands that are not consistent with the priorities and focus for your school.

7

TAKING ACTION

Supporting New Practices

Julie arrived mid-year as principal at a primary school that had little experience with collaborative inquiry. For the first two months, she worked hard with her new team to lay the groundwork for shared inquiry. Her staff was cautiously curious yet tentative about getting involved, as they weren't used to learning together and to opening up their practice.

Small conversations with each teacher about their interests were a key part of Julie's process. So was using the arts to generate curiosity. Working with the Grade 3/4 teacher, she talked with the class about the ways in which a spiral image could symbolize their learning. This class then created their own images and wrote about what the spiral meant to them. Alex, an 8-year-old student, wrote "Spirals never stop, just like my learning never stops." The artwork and writing were posted at the entrance of the school and generated a lot of discussion. The staff were ready to start some initial scanning, and an inquiry leadership team was put in place.

After some thorough scanning, a lot of dialogue about possible focus areas, and a number of hunches being surfaced, the staff landed on critical thinking as their focus for the following school year. They began to explore visible thinking strategies, and even though there were only six weeks left in the year, staff members agreed to try out one new thinking strategy with their learners. They had practised three different strategies at a professional learning meeting. They watched a short video of a class using the strategies, and they had the chance to work together in a small group of their choice to design their approach. The inquiry team had promised terrific refreshments for the "talk about it after we have tried something" half-hour meeting coming up in two weeks. Action stations!

THE SPIRAL OF Inquiry is about learning, change, and impact. The Taking Action stage begins when teams start to put into practice new ideas and strategies that will make a real difference to learners.

As teachers, we are naturally action-oriented. We see a problem and we want to fix it. For some of you, it will be a relief to know that now you are actually going to be trying something different. In fact, we are sure that many of you have already started to take action based on what you have heard from your learners and from the discussions you have had with your colleagues. Good for you!

Throughout this book, however, we have been emphasizing the importance of slowing down our predisposition to *rapid action* in order to take more *informed action*, with a greater likelihood of impact over the long term. Taking action with the Spiral doesn't just mean trying something new. It also means seeking to understand why some practices in some contexts seem to be more effective than others. You will be taking new action and looking for impact at the same time. Leadership teams will also be thinking hard about how to create the conditions where teachers feel supported in changing long-held practices. In this chapter, we invite you and your team to think about the following:

1. Creating the conditions for informed action
2. Getting started and building momentum for change
3. Sustaining action and commitment

CREATING THE CONDITIONS FOR INFORMED ACTION

In the last chapter, we asked you to consider the concept of adult stages of development and encouraged you to incorporate strategies that will meet the varied needs of your colleagues. Individuals will be at different places in their readiness for change, and this will impact readiness from a whole-school perspective.

Some schools come to Spirals with a positive mindset about professional learning. Their learning cultures are sophisticated, and their use of time and protocols are productive. Adding the Spirals framework to their work allows them to be even more powerful in their change processes.

Other schools may be in more challenging situations. Whether through high staff turnover, frequent leadership changes, top-down accountability systems, or the non-existence of collaborative practices, staff members have become discouraged and skeptical about change. In schools with battered cultures, the leadership team may have to take some time to build the motivation, sense of purpose, and feelings of efficacy that are required for informed action to take hold.

Regardless of the degree to which a school is struggling, there are almost always some positive practices in place. A recent report from a government review agency in Aotearoa/New Zealand pointed out that in many of their schools, new leadership teams had not taken the requisite time to examine what was working well.[1] This meant that the staff lacked awareness of the link between their previous efforts and their genuine successes.

Taking an appreciative approach to what *is* working in a school is a good place to start. This must be done in a way that is sincere, specific, and evidence-informed. Leaders must be seen as being trustworthy, honest, and open. Rebuilding a toxic culture takes time—but it can be done.

Recognizing the role of emotion in the change process is key to figuring out how to reduce negative feelings (see chapter 6). According to *Leading Professional Learning*, by Helen Timperley and her colleagues, uncertainty and reluctance to engage in new learning—or to make changes in practice—generally connect to one of the following dimensions: relationships, knowledge, purpose, organization, and evidence.[2]

Relationships and knowledge. Relationships can be a core source of uncertainty in collaborative inquiry work if teachers aren't confident that they will be supported in risk-taking. Teachers can experience uncertainty about both the content and processes of professional learning. They may wonder whether they have the skills and the knowledge required to make changes in their practice.

Purpose, organization, and evidence. Teachers may also feel reluctant to engage if there is a lack of clarity about the reason for new learning and if they have doubts about whether it will be positive for their learners. Inadequate organizational processes such as scheduling and resources can also contribute to reluctance. Finally, some teachers worry about the impact on their workload and wonder about whether student learning will actually improve if they try something new.

Understanding these sources of uncertainty and specifically addressing them can help leadership teams moving into the Taking Action stage of the Spiral. Ensuring that there are useful and easily accessible new resources at the first professional learning session is almost always a smart way to start.

Degrees of risk. Having tools to identity the perceptions of risk and willingness to change can also be useful as you prepare for taking action. It can be helpful to find out what particular aspects of professional learning lead to the greatest feelings of uncertainty. The six statements in the chart on the following page have been adapted and selected from a longer survey that may be found in *Leading Professional Learning.*[3]

Consider selecting a few statements and taking some time at a staff meeting to ask teachers to respond anonymously. Simply identifying areas of concern can be the starting point in developing greater willingness to give a new form of professional learning a go. Sharing the results and making sense of them together as soon as possible can be just what is needed to increase understanding and willingness to change.

STATEMENT	EXTENT TO WHICH I AM WILLING TO DO THIS					EXTENT TO WHICH I SEE THIS AS A RISK				
	Not willing				Very willing	No risk				High risk
1. Analyzing and interpreting my student outcomes with colleagues and school leaders	1	2	3	4	5	1	2	3	4	5
2. Sharing my beliefs and hunches with colleagues as part of an inquiry process	1	2	3	4	5	1	2	3	4	5
3. Participating in collaborative inquiry with colleagues I don't know well	1	2	3	4	5	1	2	3	4	5
4. Challenging the views of my colleagues in front of others when our views differ	1	2	3	4	5	1	2	3	4	5
5. Trying new teaching practices without certainty that current outcomes will improve	1	2	3	4	5	1	2	3	4	5
6. Teaching in front of my colleagues as I begin to make changes in my practice	1	2	3	4	5	1	2	3	4	5

The importance of leadership

The role of formal leaders is important at every stage in the inquiry process—and it is at the Taking Action stage that leadership becomes especially critical. Leaders can influence the outcomes of professional learning through their direct participation and through their interactions. Knowing about an individual teacher's tolerance of uncertainty and level of trust in the learning tasks they are being asked to engage in will help leaders build confidence in that teacher.

A major longitudinal study on trust in schools identified four key elements of trust:

- personal regard—knowing your teachers as individuals
- respect—listening to differing points of view
- integrity—following through on your commitments and keeping your word
- competence—ensuring core responsibilities are well managed[4]

It isn't the case that first you build trust and then you move to action. Trust is built *through* action. One of the critical determinants of trust is the ability of leaders to deal with difficult issues in respectful ways. Leadership teams that put off dealing with tough issues will find it difficult to build trust and respect in their school.

Sometimes educators avoid disagreement out of fear of offending and, as a result, a culture of niceness develops. Viviane Robinson and her colleagues argue that open-to-learning leadership provides a way of developing a culture of openness and critical challenge. "A culture of openness makes it a norm to inquire and question rather than 'nod in disagreement' while being afraid to question assumptions for fear of upsetting others."[5]

Creating the conditions for new action requires leadership that moves beyond niceness to a place that allows for challenging and important conversations. These conversations need to be handled in a way that shows care for the individual and respect for the work.

Being aware of the importance of trust is a constant challenge. Leadership teams will build trust and demonstrate their support for change by immersing themselves in new learning alongside teachers, engaging in genuine learning conversations, challenging assumptions, and trying out new practices themselves.

GETTING STARTED—AND BUILDING MOMENTUM FOR CHANGE

As Julie was laying the groundwork for inquiry in her new school, she was intentional in acknowledging the positive practices she saw in each of the classes she visited. She made a point of talking to learners at every opportunity—on the playground, in the lunch room, in the learning commons, and in their classrooms—about what they were learning and why it was important. She routinely expressed appreciation and made sure teachers heard the positive comments of their learners. She knew she had to find ways to engage some discouraged staff members. Her motto for those first few months became "Relentless kindness matters."

In every school, there are learners who are thriving, engaged, happy, and successful. Just as we need to understand what is going on for learners who are struggling, there is much to be learned from learners who are succeeding. One of the most effective ways that we have seen to spark the curiosity of teachers is through the views and voices of their learners.

A few years ago, we visited a primary school in New South Wales that was just getting started on their Spiral journey. They had started by asking the key social-emotional questions: "Can you name two adults in this building who believe you will be a success in life?" and "How do they show you?"

The deputy principal had a warm, friendly relationship with the students. They liked her and were receptive when she asked them if she could ask them a couple of important questions. Over the course of a week, she videoed a half dozen young learners' responses. At the start of the staff's first full inquiry team meeting, she played the video.

The comments from the learners were specific, honest, and moving. "He told me that I could be a good leader and that I might make a great teacher someday." "She said that she believed in me and she showed me how I am getting better." "He always smiles at me and says my name." In the three minutes it took to show the video, we watched teachers sit up taller, smile, and nod appreciatively at each other.

This became a routine way to start each inquiry meeting. It created a culture of trust and openness amongst the staff that led them to much deeper places in their own learning. When we visited the school two years later, we found the inquiry process thriving. A large area in the school was set aside as a space to make the staff's professional learning visible. It was filled with examples from students about how their learning was being impacted by the staff focus on building learner agency.

The leadership team described this space as a learning "canvas" for their important change work. Teachers, students, family members, and visitors to the school were able to see tangible evidence that learner agency was growing. The staff began each of their weekly meetings with good news stories about their Spirals work. We were impressed that good news included acknowledging risk-taking, mistake-making, lessons learned, uncertainties, and learner outcomes. Smart routines.

In addition to using the voices of learners to build commitment, providing opportunities for teachers to share the positive practices that are already working in the focus area of the team inquiry can be encouraging and motivating. Short presentations at staff meetings, lunch and learn sessions, gallery walks through classrooms, and visible samples of high-quality student work can all help to reduce anxiety and fear of change.

And never forget the motivational aspect of providing good food. One of the most enticing ways we have seen of engaging teachers with trying new approaches and sharing their practice was at a small rural school in northern British Columbia (BC). Every Friday morning the principal arrived and placed a large pot of soup to simmer on the stove in the staff room. All morning the aroma wafted through the hallway. The teachers who agreed to join him in a lunch meeting got to savour the soup and left with some new strategies about how to use the natural setting around the school to teach scientific concepts outdoors.

Using available time wisely

Harvard researchers Kathryn Parker Boudett and Elizabeth A. City, in their resource *Meeting Wise: Making the Most of Collaborative Time for Educators,* note that, when they "ask people what gets in the way of improving learning and teaching, 'time' is consistently one of the top three responses .... Time—especially time for adults to learn together—is a precious resource." No one likes to have their time wasted, and having to sit through a dull meeting at the end of a busy day can be deeply frustrating. Fortunately, as we learn in *Meeting Wise*, "while the research base on the use of time is not deep, one finding is clear: *quality matters more than quantity*."[6]

Quantity, however, does matter to some degree. In many situations, however, the focus needs to shift from "Do we have enough time?" to "Are we making the best use of the time we have available?"

Leadership teams need to think carefully about how and when to structure meetings focused on new actions. We have found that a regular rhythm of sixty- to ninety-minute meetings scheduled during the school day at two- to three-week intervals is optimal in most settings. There needs to be enough time for new actions to be tried but not so much time that the sense of urgency is diminished.

In some contexts, this time is built into the school schedule. Schools with limited resources may find it a challenge to provide time for teacher learning during the day. Nevertheless, we have seen many creative approaches that honour local contexts and respect the need for teachers to have a chance to learn when they are rested.

After the first couple of months at her school, by using school-based resources carefully, Julie introduced the notion of Thirds days. Once every six weeks all teachers (in small groups) were able to meet for a third of the day to review scanning information, to surface hunches, and to have open conversations about what their next steps needed to be. The inquiry leadership team co-designed the meetings, and the staff appreciated meeting during the day. They also valued Julie's presence at each of the meetings, as she kept track of the new understandings that were surfaced and the agreements to action that were made.

Designing productive meetings

Involving staff in designing meetings at the Taking Action stage of the Spiral can build commitment and increase accountability. Little will squash enthusiasm for proposed changes more than poorly organized, unfocused meetings that feel like a waste of time. You might consider asking team members to respond to the following prompts:

1. Think of the worst meeting you have ever attended. Take two minutes to write down everything that made it unproductive.
2. Think of the best meeting you've ever attended. What made it so great? Take another two minutes to jot down ideas.

Use the responses to develop an agreement about what makes for a good meeting. Then use this agreement as a guide in your planning and as a way of generating feedback at the end of each session.

Generally, there are four key aspects of any effective meeting: purpose, process, preparation, and pacing. Here is a checklist from *Meeting Wise* that can help your teams in planning:

	MEETING CHECKLIST	YES	NO
PURPOSE	1. Have we identified clear and important meeting ***objectives*** that contribute to the goal of improved learning in our area?		
	2. Have we established the ***connection*** between the work of this and other meetings in the series?		
PROCESS	3. Have we incorporated ***feedback*** from previous meetings?		
	4. Have we designed challenging ***activities*** that advance the meeting objectives and engage all participants?		
	5. Have we assigned ***roles***, including facilitator, timekeeper and note taker?		
	6. Have we built in time to identify and commit to ***next steps***?		
	7. Have we built in time for ***assessment*** of what worked and what didn't in the meeting?		
PREPARATION	8. Have we gathered or developed ***materials*** (drafts, charts, etc.) that will help to focus and advance the meeting objectives?		
	9. Have we determined what, if any, ***pre-work*** we will ask participants to do prior to the meeting?		
PACING	10. Have we put *time allocations* to each activity on the agenda?		
	11. Have we ensured that we will address the *primary objective* early in the meeting?		
	12. Is it *realistic* to expect to get through our agenda in the time allocated?		

Boudette, K. P., City, E. A. (2014). *Meeting Wise: Making the Most of Collaborative Time for Educators*, p. 166. Cambridge, MA: Harvard Education Press. Reprinted with permission.

Seeing this in practice

What does this look like in practice? Here is what we saw at a large Australian primary school. The staff were dissatisfied with the progress of their learners in developing mathematical understandings. They had observed that some of their learners seemed to tune out during math lessons and that learner responses to the cognitive questions were often quite superficial. They had a hunch that the way they approached teaching math was somewhat uninspiring, and that they really needed some new approaches.

The staff started the learning and action stages by agreeing to meet in teams of six teachers every two weeks for ninety minutes. The school had a healthy professional learning budget that allowed them to contract with local facilitators who arranged outdoor learning experiences while the teachers were away from their classes. Students were engaged, and teachers appreciated not having to prepare a lesson for a substitute teacher.

The teams met in a comfortable room around a large table. The principal and deputy head were full participants in each meeting, and the meetings were chaired by an enthusiastic teacher-leader with interest and skill in facilitating adult learning. There was a culture of good humour and high personal regard. Good food was served, and the coffee was strong.

The agenda for the meetings always followed the same rhythm—ten minutes of check-in to ensure every voice was heard, ten minutes of new learning about mathematical understandings, thirty minutes for lesson design in partners, thirty minutes for reporting to the group and receiving productive feedback on the lesson plans, and ten minutes to reflect on the meeting and summarize next steps.

The leadership team understood that many of the teachers were nervous about feedback and anxious about being observed by their formal leaders. As a result, they decided to focus on team lesson design, team teaching, and team critique. Teachers agreed to work in pairs to review how their lessons went and to report at the next meeting what changes they were making as a result of their partnerships. This action-learning cycle was repeated many times.

What made things work in this school was the leadership of the principal and her deputies, the attention to detail of the inquiry team in planning the meetings, the infusion of new learning in right-sized chunks, and the confidence among the teachers that they would be supported in trying out new approaches.

Give it a go

Previously (chapter 6) we have talked about designing learning sessions to meet the needs of teachers at various stages of development—from instrumental to self-transforming ways of knowing. We have also introduced you (also in chapter 6) to the idea of symmetry between the ways adults learn and the ways in which students are taught.

Moving to action requires putting into practice new strategies, reflecting on what is working, and adapting and adjusting along the way. Things hardly ever work out perfectly when trying something for the first time. Many teachers have been socialized to avoid mistakes, which makes trying out new strategies a bit risky.

We were struck by the Flop Friday approach taken in one Australian secondary school. Every Friday afternoon the staff agreed to meet, often at a coffee shop or pub, to share one thing they had tried that week that had genuinely flopped. They shared a few laughs and then discussed what changes they would make the following week. Making it normal to have "flops" and to learn from them provided a great example of a collective growth mindset in action.

Others have also recognized that "encouraging people to try new or difficult things, without worrying" about the initial results working perfectly, "gives them the confidence to step out of their comfort zone."[7] By sharing stories of strategies that went awry and then figuring out how to regroup, individuals can lose their understandable fear of criticism.

In Finland, the idea of celebrating mistakes has developed into a National Day for Failure.[8] This was initiated in 2010 by a group of university students who recognized their country "would be needing thousands of new businesses and jobs in the future." They saw that a "fear of inadequacy was holding many people back from founding those businesses or pursuing those jobs."[9] They were determined to make celebrating mistakes an integral part of learning. Let's learn from the Finns. Let's not use the fear of failure or criticism to hold us back from trying something new.

SUSTAINING ACTION AND COMMITMENT

Once you have agreed to try out new approaches, then you need to consider ways to sustain the momentum, especially when things inevitably get tricky. In this final section, we will share some of the strategies that we have seen work effectively in different schools. We hope some of these will be of interest to you and your team.

Learner feedback and making learning visible

One of the most powerful sources of information throughout the Spiral process is our learners. We encourage teams to stay in that place of curiosity where they are consistently asking, "What's going on for our learners?" and "How do we know?" Involving learners directly in meetings where new strategies are being discussed, helping them understand the reasons for the changes, and then reporting back on how it is going can help keep everyone on track.

We have mentioned previously the power of capturing learner feedback on video and starting staff meetings with positive reflections from learners. We were also impressed by the staff of one high school who took seriously the idea of listening to learners about classroom lesson designs. After their initial scanning, the inquiry team made increasing learner agency their central focus. They came up with a practical approach that every staff member agreed to try. On Friday afternoons every staff member asked the learners in their last class to write answers to two questions: *What worked for you this week in the learning we did together? What is one idea that would make the learning even better for you next week?*

The staff agreed that, before they left for the weekend, they would read what their learners had to say and then build into the following week one idea or strategy that had been suggested. They made their commitment clear to their learners at the start of the next week. This clear area of focus and simple strategy was successful in transforming the culture of the school. The staff became accustomed to seeking feedback about learning and teaching from their students and went on to develop a school-wide focus on highly engaging pedagogy combined with learner agency.

Making learning visible through student displays, presentations, bulletin boards, and web and blog posts also helps to sustain action and commitment. Many inquiry teams, especially those focused on critical thinking, are finding the resources from Ron Ritchhart and his colleagues particularly helpful. We encourage you to take a look at both their first resource, *Making Thinking Visible* (2011), and their second book, *The Power of Making Thinking Visible* (2020). The strategies they describe have all been extensively field tested—they are practical and theoretically sound.

One of the most impressive primary schools we have visited is in Brisbane. A regional network symposium was held at the school. Highly articulate student guides toured us through the school and pointed out the visible thinking strategies in action in every classroom. This school was highly influenced by the routines outlined in *Making Thinking Visible*. They also worked with and were coached by Kath Murdoch. Her first book, *The Power of Inquiry*, provides a number of great strategies for elementary school teams whose focus is on deepening student curiosity and engagement. Her most recent book, *Getting Personal With Inquiry Learning*, includes a wide range of examples from schools where personalized inquiry is transforming the experiences of young learners. Regardless of your focus area, drawing on learner feedback and making sure that the new learning of both staff and students is made highly visible are motivators for sustained action.

TeachMeets

A TeachMeet is an organized but informal way for teachers to share good practice in micro-presentations. Although these can be conducted online with teachers from around the world participating, the concept of quick sharing works well at the school level too. Building in regular times for two or three teachers to share new practices or to illustrate the use of a new learning technology app in very short presentations can be just the spark that is needed to sustain motivation.

We saw an example of this at a northern England secondary school that had dramatically improved their results over a three-year period. Every Wednesday before school there was a ten-minute "catching up on what is happening" staff meeting. During this time, one staff member would take three minutes to explain something new they were trying that was working better for their students. The focus was on sharing strategies that other teachers could try relatively easily.

Then, once a term, the whole staff met in a local pub after school. Over snacks and beverages, eight staff members presented their work to their colleagues in three-minute bursts. The teachers we talked to said they found these early evening sessions both practical and inspiring. The TeachMeets created a "can-do spirit" about new practices and helped build a school-wide culture of continuous learning.

Ignite sessions

A bit more formal than TeachMeets, an Ignite session consists of one presenter sharing exactly twenty slides that automatically advance every fifteen seconds.[10] The result is a short, sharp presentation that lasts five minutes. The topic is always about something the presenter is passionate about sharing. We have attended many Ignite presentations, and each one has left us intrigued and inspired as educators.

Changing up the venue for both TeachMeets and Ignite sessions can build in novelty and sustain interest. We have attended and hosted learning events virtually as well as in person in local coffee shops, bookstores, restaurants, art galleries, community centres, and outdoor settings.

When inviting educators to share their work through a TeachMeet or an Ignite session, consider asking a range of teachers to share. This is not about always shining a light on the stars. It is about opening up practices, respecting where people are at, and having some fun in the process.

Teaching sprints

Many schools have had success with using short action sprints[11] to build momentum. You might consider the inner loop of the spiral to represent a teaching sprint within the Taking Action stage.

Sprints allow teacher teams to work together on big changes by breaking the work into smaller, time-defined chunks. Used as an approach within a longer-term inquiry, sprints provide inquiry teams the chance to experience the impact of actions over short cycles. This allows new learning to become embedded in classroom practice and lets team members see the results quickly—in anywhere from one to three weeks. According to Simon Breakspear and Bronwyn Jones, there are three key phases to what they term a "teaching sprint":

1. **Prepare: Come together to determine a focus for practice improvement**
   In this phase, teachers:
   - Engage in new learning informed by research evidence
   - Draw out connections and challenges to practice
   - Determine a precise strategy/technique for practice improvement.
2. **Sprint: Intentionally practise in classrooms**
   Over two to four weeks, teachers:
   - Intentionally practise the chosen strategy/technique in classrooms
   - Make adjustments, in light of what's happening
   - Check in with colleagues to sustain momentum
3. **Review: Reflect on the process and learn from each other**
   In this phase, teachers:
   - Reflect on the effectiveness of the sprint
   - Share insights and determine implications for future practice
   - Identify possible next steps for professional learning[12]

Key to the notion of sprints is the quick process of trying out new actions to develop adaptive expertise. Continually coming back to the key questions of "What is going on for our learners?" and "How do we know?" will ensure that your quick actions are consistent with the overall focus of improving the experiences of your learners.

Wise counsel for inquiry actions

Wise counsel is a strategy that we have found particularly useful in addressing practical problems that inevitably surface as new approaches are tried. By using a well-defined, carefully timed protocol, teachers have the opportunity to draw on the expertise of their colleagues efficiently and safely. Participants serving as wise counsel often become genuinely invested in the challenge their colleague is experiencing. Trust and openness grow. New strategies are surfaced.

The protocol starts with one person presenting a problem of practice to a small group of four to five colleagues. The presenter then listens carefully to their colleagues as they provide suggestions and feedback over a relatively short period of time. A key part of the protocol is that, after outlining the problem, the presenter physically turns his or her back, thus avoiding eye contact with the discussants.[13] The more teams become familiar with the protocol, the more effectively it can be used to generate strategies, open up thinking, build trust, and strengthen teamwork.

Celebrations of learning

Setting a regular time during the school year when staff gather to share their learning has become a central feature of the inquiry schools we visit. Sometimes these can take the form of a gallery walk where teachers share visual representations of their work. Sometimes learners take the lead in explaining what has been accomplished. Sometimes schools create short videos to show their progress. Often families are invited to view the new learning. Celebrating progress, regardless of how small the steps initially appear to be, is an important way to sustain momentum. We'll return to the importance of celebration in chapter 8.

By this point it should be clear that taking action is a team sport, not a solo activity. The challenge to leadership teams is to ensure that there are opportunities for everyone to share ideas, to support each other when the going inevitably gets tough, and to celebrate successes along the way, no matter how small. This means structuring opportunities for dialogue, designing well-organized meetings, providing time for observation and reflection, and creating the conditions for second, third, and fourth tries without fear of judgment or fear of failure.

A REMINDER ABOUT TAKING ACTION:

Taking Action Is

- Learning more deeply about new ways of doing things—and then trying them out
- Seeking a deep understanding of why proposed new practices are more effective than others
- Evaluating the impact of the actions on learning

- Seeking feedback directly from learners about how the changes are going for them
- Continuing to build trust and acknowledging feelings of vulnerability

Taking Action Is Not

- Trying something new without first considering its value and relevance to your situation
- Applying new strategies without monitoring the effects on your learners
- Assuming that everyone feels fine about the changes involved

BIG IDEAS FROM CHAPTER 7

- Leadership teams create the conditions for informed action.
- The thoughtful use of time and well-designed meetings will help build trust and momentum for change.
- Trust is built through action.
- Acknowledge and celebrate small steps.

FREQUENTLY ASKED QUESTIONS ABOUT TAKING ACTION

How do you respond to the comment, "I tried it [i.e., a new strategy] and it didn't work"?

Rarely does everything go smoothly the first time. Let's not use an initial failure as a reason to stop trying. Our answer would be to probe gently to understand more about the context, what exactly was tried, with whom, and under what circumstances, to find out more about what went awry.

One strategy that we have used ourselves and have seen used elsewhere is for a member of the leadership team to offer to try the strategy out with the teacher's own class and have the teacher provide feedback on what did and didn't work.

This shift in the balance of power can lead to new insights and deeper understanding on the part of both individuals involved.

Learners also need to understand the purpose for the change. Getting their feedback on what worked and didn't work is a way to build learner agency and develop a learning culture. The key here is to support the teacher to try again without judgment or fear of failure.

You talk a lot about teachers. What about the role of education assistants in the inquiry process?

This is such an important question. Contractual agreements for paraprofessionals differ across jurisdictions, and sometimes these agreements make it tricky for education assistants to participate in meetings that take place outside of their regular hours. It is really important that everyone on the staff—education assistants, cultural support workers, the office staff, the custodial staff, the cafeteria supervisors—understands the direction for the school and can talk about it knowledgably.

A key role for the inquiry leadership team is to ensure that everyone is included as much as possible. Short meetings, regular conversations at times convenient to the support staff, and open invitations to participate in learning events and staff gatherings are a starting place. Education assistants, in addition to understanding the purpose of the actions that are underway, need to be supported in developing the skills required to help make the shifts. Think about what you can do in your setting to create the conditions where everyone is included, involved, and respected for the contribution they are making.

QUESTIONS FOR LEARNING CONVERSATIONS

1. How will you engage your colleagues in ensuring professional learning meetings are well designed, action-oriented, and meet the needs of each participant?
2. How will you use student voice and student feedback to build commitment to learning actions and to keep the focus on what is most important?
3. How might you use short sprints of action to create and sustain momentum?

4. What are some creative ways to share the results of new learning that might work in your context?

5. How and when will you celebrate the new actions you are taking? Will you include learners? Their families? Some community members?

LEADERSHIP MOVES

- Taking action is not just about the changes teachers will make to their practice. As a formal leader, be open and transparent about the changes YOU are making yourself. Share what is working, where you are struggling, and what you are doing about it.
- Never assume that everyone is on board. Check in frequently with your staff. Don't let the important conversations take place in the parking lot. Bring them into the meeting room.
- Ask for feedback yourself—from staff and from learners—about the ways in which you are supporting risk-taking and changes in practice. Listen carefully then act on what you have heard.

8

CHECKING

Assessing for Impact

The staff at MJ Secondary School had worked hard to come to an agreement that learning is no longer only about what students know. It is also about their level of understanding and what they can do with what they know. The staff then developed a specific focus on building stronger connections between what students are learning in their classrooms and real-world applications. They have also been focused on increasing student motivation and agency through a school-wide focus on assessment for learning, and many teachers have moved to comment-only feedback. Letter grades are no longer the main event.

Teachers have agreed that their initial shared goal was that at the end of every class every student would be able to answer the following questions: "What did I learn today?" "Why did I learn it?" "How does this connect to the world outside of school?" "How will this learning help me in the future?"

Staff have been checking in regularly with individual learners. They have also held a series of focus groups with 150 students from Grades 8 to 12 four times during the year. It is now almost the end of the school year, and it is time to check—to figure out how much difference they are making overall.

BY THIS POINT in the Spiral, as a team you have scanned your students and selected a specific area of focus. You have reflected on your own actions—positive, neutral, or negative—that have led to the current situation for your learners. You have been immersed in new learning, and you have designed new learning opportunities for your colleagues. You have been trying out new approaches and new strategies. You have constantly been asking yourselves, "What is going on for our learners?" and "How do we know?" You have been listening to your learners and reflecting on their feedback.

You have seen eyes light up when a new concept becomes clear. You have witnessed learners encouraging each other through difficult tasks. You have seen reluctant readers find joy through books. You have heard from parents how much their child is benefitting from the chance to explore an area of interest in greater depth. You have been gratified by the depth of the questions posed by your learners to the Elder in Residence. You have seen lonely and anxious students gaining confidence and making friends. You take delight in the smiles and laughter that fill the hallways, the classrooms, and the playgrounds. And you have wondered why some of your learners continue to struggle.

Explicitly or not, you have been checking throughout the Spiral. Whether you and your team selected a unit, a term, a semester, or a year as the frame for your inquiry, the Checking stage is the point at which you need to stand back and ask yourselves, "Are we making enough of a difference?"

One of the challenges for inquiry teams just starting out is to figure out what evidence will help answer this question. This is why, in chapter 3, we emphasized the importance of getting clear on what difference you want to make—and what evidence you will use to determine progress—early on at the Focusing stage of the Spiral.

In this chapter, we will explore the idea of evaluative thinking and why an inquiry stance is especially critical when examining evidence of student learning. We will also provide some examples of the kinds of evidence that teachers find most compelling—evidence that is close to the learners.

WHAT IS EVALUATIVE THINKING?

The Checking stage of the Spiral requires a clear-eyed and disciplined approach to determining the extent to which the desired outcomes for learners are being realized. Teams need to bring an evaluative thinking mindset to this question. In "Evaluative Thinking for Successful Educational Innovation," a working paper commissioned by the Organisation for Economic Co-operation and Development (OECD), Lorna Earl and Helen Timperley draw on the work of Gavin Bennett and Nasreen Jessani (2011) as they provide this definition:

> Evaluative thinking is a means of thinking, of viewing the world. An ongoing process of questioning, reflecting, learning and modifying. Evaluative thinking is an inherently reflective process, a means of resolving the "creative tension" between our current and desired levels of performance. It allows us to define the lessons we want to learn, to determine the means for capturing those lessons, and to design systems to apply them in improving our performance. By going beyond the more time- and activity-bound process of monitoring and evaluation, evaluative thinking is learning for change.[1]

An ongoing challenge for inquiry leadership teams is to be clear on what evidence sources will be most useful for determining impact. Throughout this book we have stressed the importance of listening to learners as a key evidence source. In many jurisdictions, "evidence" is a code word for formal test results or other sources that are perceived to be "objective" or "hard." While these sources have a role, schools also have access to many rich sources of data that are often not well used. "Evaluative Thinking for Successful Educational Innovation" also cautions that "the challenge of using evidence well is to identify what evidence is available and what more needs to be collected, analysed and interpreted to identify if things are on the right track."[2]

Selecting evidence sources that are directly linked to the focus area is key. If your team is concentrating on learner agency, how will you know that learners are increasingly taking ownership of their learning? If your focus is on self-regulation, what evidence will you look for that learners are developing and applying a range of new strategies? If improving the decision-making processes of your learners is your focus, how will you know they are actually making better decisions? If you are focused on improving well-being and connectedness, what will tell you that you are on the right track?

To practice evaluative thinking, inquiry teams need to know how to select and use evidence to make the changes that will impact student outcomes. Teams must also be able to suspend judgment and make fewer assumptions when considering the evidence that has been gathered. Deirdre Le Fevre and her colleagues suggest that inquiry teams engaged in evaluative thinking continually ask themselves the following questions: "What evidence is there for this claim?" "How good is this evidence?" And, "What other evidence or explanations might be considered?"[3]

There is a difference between gathering evidence and interpreting it. It is only when we make sense of numbers, facts, and stories that they become useful. The first step is to gather the evidence and organize it in a way that is accessible for all the staff. The next step is to provide some scaffolding for teachers to know what questions to ask about the evidence. Then there needs to be time for teachers to work in teams to make sense of it all. As you do this in a thoughtful way, staff members will develop collective ownership for what the evidence reveals. The last step is to celebrate what you've accomplished.

The Checking stage isn't about "proving" that everything has worked. It's about being open and curious about what *has* worked, for whom and under what conditions. The word "enough" is critical. Is it *enough* for some learners to be thriving while others continue to struggle? We think not. This is equity thinking in action.

Being open to a critical analysis of where things are at for learners at the end of a Spiral requires teams to have a genuine inquiry and evidence-seeking mindset. This is not the time for blame, shame, or fame. It's the time to consider how far you have come as a team—and what your next moves might be. It's also the time to pause and celebrate the gains you have made.

But let's take a look at the first three steps that we'll take on our way to those celebrations.

STEP 1: GATHER AND ORGANIZE EVIDENCE

There are a few different forms of evidence that teachers in inquiry schools are finding helpful.

Big data and small data

It can be tempting when looking for ways to determine impact to rely exclusively on easily available data gathered through standardized assessments or student surveys. Data from large-scale assessments usually don't provide the kind of specific and nuanced information that helps teachers make better decisions at the classroom level.

Finnish educator Pasi Sahlberg is currently a professor of education policy at the University of New South Wales. He has worked as a policy advisor for countries around the world, and one of the recurring themes in his talks and publications is the need to balance big data with small data. What does this mean?

In "Small Data for Big Change: What Does It Mean for Teachers?" this expert on educational assessment explains that international student assessments, provincial or state assessments, large-scale satisfaction surveys, and national education statistics are examples of big data. "As masses of student testing data grow, so does the desire to harvest it for patterns."[4] However, "standardized tests or opinion surveys may help to identify some general trends but they are not able to reveal the deep secrets of pedagogy."[5] According to "Small Data for Big Change," teachers value and understand "the importance of human observations, face-to-face conversations and critical reflections in making sense of what goes on in classrooms."[6] We agree with this.

Evidence needs to be usable and useful. In *Leading Professional Learning: Practical Strategies for Impact in Schools,* Helen Timperley and her colleagues explain that usable evidence is accessible, readable, and ethically stored and distributed, with the information matched to the learner. Useful evidence provides information about valued outcomes connected to the questions and focus areas of the school. As school staffs often feel swamped by big data, there is an increasing need to shift the focus to small data. This is the kind of information that helps teachers understand those aspects of learning and teaching that are less easily measurable. It is small data that can help teachers understand in a timely way why some students are thriving while others are struggling. The closer the evidence is to the action of teaching and learning, the more compelling it is for teachers.

Another way of thinking about small data has been introduced by American educator Shane Safir, in her book *The Listening Leader*. Let's briefly explore what she means by street data and what the implications are for inquiry teams at the Checking stage.

Street data

In *The Listening Leader*, we learn that "much of the data that we need is right before us if we choose to listen."[7] This book's description of three increasingly granular levels of data helps illuminate the importance of using close-to-the-learner evidence at the Checking stage of the Spiral.

Level 1: Satellite data

Satellite data have a large-grain size. They help indicate patterns of student achievement and equity and point us in a general direction for further investigation. Evidence of student learning includes standardized test scores, provincial or state assessments, and graduation rates.

Level 2: Map data

Map data have a medium-grain size. They help identify reading, math, and other skill challenges and point us in a slightly more focused direction. Evidence of student learning includes student perception surveys, oral fluency assessments, and performance-based assessments.

Level 3: Street data

Street data are fine grained. They help identify specific student misconceptions and monitor internalization of key skills. They inform and shape our next moves. Gathering this kind of data requires careful listening and observation. Evidence of student learning includes non-verbal cues, student interviews and focus group information, one-on-one running records, student work artifacts, and teacher observations of students engaged in specific activities.

In *Street Data: A Next Generation Model for Equity, Pedagogy and School Transformation*, Shane Safir and Jamila Dugan challenge educators to consider why there is such an overreliance on satellite and map data. They argue that street forms of data can be humanizing, liberating, and healing.[8] This work links the power of street data to the courage required to take an anti-racist stance. An anti-racist stance starts with deep listening to understand the experiences of another. This means listening deeply to young people whose voices have often not been heard.

One of the big lessons that we have learned through our work with inquiry schools is never to ask a question if you aren't prepared to act on what you hear. You will build trust with vulnerable individuals and communities when they can see that you are not only listening respectfully but also prepared to act on what they have to say.

It can be tempting when designing a survey to add all kinds of questions—some more relevant than others. You may have experienced survey fatigue yourself when responding to an opinion poll or completing a feedback survey from a recent travel experience. A helpful guideline is only to ask questions of your learners and their families if you are ready to take action on the responses. Surveys that contain three or four carefully crafted questions are often much more useful than lengthy surveys with dozens of questions.

At the beginning of the Spiral, we asked you to start by asking a few key questions of your learners. You have been seeking out their voices throughout the whole process. The Checking stage now brings you back to the questions that informed the Scanning process in the first place.

The two key Scanning questions: Checking continually

Can you name two adults who believe you will be a success in life?

At the beginning of the Spiral process, we asked you to interview learners in response to two specific questions. You want to find out if there are any learners who are not able to connect with and name an adult in the building who believes in their success. And you also want to know that every learner understands the purpose and relevance of what they are learning—as well as how they are doing.

We have talked earlier about the importance of moving to action right away with those students who do not feel connected or supported. The goal is to ensure that 100% of your learners are able to name at least two adults in the school who believe in their future success and that all of your learners are able to describe the specific behaviours of the adults that convey this belief. Gathering this data at the beginning of the Spiral and throughout the process will give you a clear idea at the Checking stage of the progress you are making and the work that remains to be done.

In the Scanning stage, one secondary school identified fifty students who couldn't name anyone who believed in them. In addition to a number of staff members engaging in the 2 x 10 strategy (see chapter 2), the leadership team started every staff meeting with a photo of one of these students. The picture was used to generate a brainstormed list of all the positive characteristics of this young person. It didn't take long to do and was a great reminder of the importance of keeping learners at the centre of all decisions. By the end of the year, the number of disconnected students was dramatically reduced.

What are you learning and why is it important?

Many inquiry teams create their own scoring guides or rubrics as they dive more deeply into this meta-cognitive question with their learners. The Delta School District in British Columbia (BC) has set a target of ensuring that all students will demonstrate an understanding of themselves as learners by being able to answer what they call the Big Three questions: "What am I learning?" "How is it going?" "What are my next steps?"[9]

They have collected video samples of students responding to these questions, and teachers have developed a continuum of response types so that they can use these student responses to check the extent to which learners are progressing toward their target. Using these questions and checking regularly is making a big difference. As one teacher in Delta said:

> These questions have completely changed my practice. Everything I do revolves around these questions—they guide my planning and my assessment, and they help me focus and consolidate my thinking. I have seen these questions change my students, as well. They help my students take ownership of their learning,

> and help them engage in their learning. My students (Grade 2/3 this year), are astonishingly good at talking about their learning and pretty bang on when it comes to assessing their strengths and stretches. By asking my students these questions, I feel like I know them better as learners, and I am better equipped to help them move their learning forward. We are starting to notice a real shift at our school, because so many of us are using these questions, and the students are getting used to talking about their learning.[10]

Another primary school identified helping learners understand the big ideas in content areas as the focus for their inquiry. Their Scanning revealed that many of their learners were passive and compliant. They were also unclear about the important concepts. The staff wanted their students not only to be more aware of the big ideas but also to be more aware of the ways in which they accessed and generated ideas themselves. The leadership team developed a four-part rubric for responses to the following questions:

1. What are you learning?
2. Why is what you are learning important?
3. What are the big ideas?
4. How do you get your ideas?

Using the categories of *emerging, developing*, and *proficient*, they were able to categorize responses from learners at different points during the Spiral and were able to track the growth in individual student responses over the term. As an example, in response to the question "How do you get your ideas?" the answers of Jamie, a boy in Grade 5, progressed from "I ask my friends" to "I look on the internet" to "From listening to other in the class. When other kids talk and share what they know, I can make new connections. This helps me out and then I can bring in my knowledge and create something bigger with them. I also get new ideas from the work we do in class and from past experiences, connections and memory." This rubric is a good example of the kind of scaffolding that is needed to help teachers make sense of the evidence they have gathered.

STEP 2: DECIDE HOW TO ASK QUESTIONS ABOUT YOUR EVIDENCE

The staff at MJ Secondary was ready to start checking more formally. Earlier in the Spiral process, they had asked students to complete a short written survey on their levels of engagement. Their next step was to survey the students again to compare their responses. They invited student focus groups to help them make sense of the responses. They also reached out to their parent community to elicit their observations about the impact of the changes they were making.

Next, they gathered a sample of comments from students connected to the key questions they had agreed on. They took a look at success rates, course completion, and work habit comments. They collected photos and video evidence of quality student work and the ways in which students were making real-world connections. As they considered all the evidence, they felt confident that they were on the right track. They also acknowledged that they still had work to do before they could be satisfied that the difference they were making was enough.

Indigenous understandings, equity, and indicators of success

Checking requires teams to ask some hard questions and to have some important conversations about what success for all learners actually means. Our goal in the BC Networks of Inquiry and Indigenous Education (NOIIE) is for every learner to cross the stage with dignity, purpose, and options. This means more than just earning a high school leaving certificate. It means that no young person has been on the receiving end of racist behaviour and that each one can see a purposeful future for themselves. It means that they have succeeded in the most challenging courses possible so that their options for post-secondary opportunities are expanded rather than diminished.

When community members in BC have been asked for evidence of success with respect to Indigenous education, there is general agreement on the use of existing measures:

- Graduation rates
- Retention rates (i.e., reduction in the drop-out rate)
- Course completion

This is a starting point, but it is not enough. In BC, the Ministry of Education's publication of *Aboriginal Worldviews and Perspectives in the Classroom: Moving Forward* (2015) was the result of broad community consultation. In addition to the agreed-upon measures listed above, this report suggests a number of other indicators that include:

- Students articulating where they are in their learning and where they are going
- Students experiencing smooth transitions between schools
- Indigenous students accessing and participating in specialized district programs at the same rate as other students
- All students graduating with an understanding of Indigenous peoples and cultures

As we strive for greater equity in our schools, we need to make sure that we are asking questions about learners who have been traditionally underserved by the school system. The issue of school exclusions in England has gained national attention.[11] In some local authorities, Black Caribbean students are excluded at a rate six times higher than their white peers. Similarly, Gypsy, Roma, and Traveler children are excluded at much higher rates. In the US, the inequities associated with the school experiences of Black, Latino, Asian, Native American, and white students have long been documented.

Regardless of the context of your school, engaging in the Spiral means that you are asking the tough questions about what is going on for different groups within your community and then looking for the kind of evidence that will indicate whether or not you are making enough of a difference for them.

Traditional indicators of school success are limited in their capacity to let us know what is actually going on at the level of the individual learner. They don't capture the global shifts from content-based to competency-focused curriculum. Let's look briefly at some emerging work that is underway to shift assessment and credentialing practices.

New competencies—New indicators of success

There is broad consensus across democratic systems that new competencies for young people are required, as Sandra Milligan and her colleagues at the Melbourne Graduate School of Education point out in their 2020 report, *Future-Proofing Students: What They Need to Know and How Educators Can Assess and Credential Them.* Whether these are called 21st-century skills, general capabilities, core competencies, or transversal skills, the goal is the same: "For students to thrive they need to become expert learners."[12]

While the focus of curriculum has shifted to include capabilities, developing new performance indicators is still a work in progress. Indicators in areas like literacy, numeracy, and the use of information and communication technology are well developed in many jurisdictions.[13] As we mentioned in the introduction, in BC educators have had access to a set of performance indicators in reading, writing, numeracy, and social responsibility for over two decades.[14] These tools have helped teachers gather important evidence of individual student growth. They have also helped create a coaching culture in our province.

The work reported in *Future-Proofing Students* provides a useful starting point for developing indicators in some key areas that are currently less developed. These are areas like communication, collaboration, and ethical behaviour. Indicators for personal skills such as persistence, and the capacity to use feedback and analytical skills, such as computational thinking, creativity and criticality, are paramount. The digital era is highlighting the need for entrepreneurial and enterprise skills.[15] New indicators are required to determine the extent to which students are gaining these skills.

Future-Proofing Students states that "The use of a developmental learner profile based on quality assessments would enable students to better manage their own learning, monitor their own progress and recognize the learning skills they already have or need to attain."[16] The authors also argue that "most capabilities for learning can be taught and assessed if conceptualized as ordered sequences of increasingly sophisticated, teachable behaviors."[17] "Intrinsic to the idea that learning capabilities should be taught and assessed is the premise that while capabilities are *learned* in context, they are . . . *transferable* by a learner from one context to another."[18]

The report contains sample progressions for collaborative problem-solving and reading development that provide a potential blueprint for assessing other complex capabilities. Without going into the fine detail, the five-strand progression for collaborative problem-solving describes six levels of attainment.[19] For schools whose focus is on collaborative problem-solving, having a framework[20] such as this to assess "participation, perspective-taking, social regulation, task regulation, and knowledge-building"[21] will be invaluable.

The work at Melbourne University[22] is breaking new ground as educators collaborate with academics to develop new metrics for school success. Other organizations such as the Brookings Institution in the US and Rethinking Assessment in England are also trying to find better approaches to developing the kinds of assessments that can capture the complete picture of who students are, what they know, and whether they are prepared to use that knowledge to advance their lives and the lives of others. In his 2021 paper, *Rethinking Assessment in Education: The Case for Change,* Bill Lucas provides a range of examples of the ways in which assessment practices are changing—and the ways they further need to change. He points to the promising work by the Australian Council for Educational Research for the progress they are making in defining and developing methods for assessing creativity and collaboration. This researcher also references the work taking place in the UK focused on developing and assessing oracy. A group of researchers at Cambridge University has developed a set of benchmarks to facilitate more precise understanding of student progression.[23]

We share these initiatives to indicate that powerful thinkers across the world are developing increasingly sophisticated ways of assessing student learning. The breakthroughs in assessment will be deeply helpful to inquiry teams tackling the complex challenges of helping students become expert learners.

STEP 3: TIME TO MAKE SENSE OF IT ALL

At MJ Secondary, the staff were pleased with the changes they saw in learner agency and engagement, and the responses on both the parent and student surveys were positive. Still they noted that there were some disparities in success rates in different subject areas, and the responses from their senior students were not as positive as those from their junior students.

They also found that there were still a handful of students who did not feel there were adults in the building who believed in them. Collectively they took a breath and paused for a couple of weeks to celebrate the growth they were seeing. Then they were ready to dive back into a new round of Scanning to get a deeper understanding of what was going on for their learners in these specific areas of concern.

There is a point at which inquiry teams will need to determine not only that you are making a difference for your learners but that you are making enough of a difference. *Enough* is the word.

What is *enough*?

Over the past decade there have been significant efforts in BC to improve the graduation rates for Indigenous learners. In some communities, the gains have been impressive. A few years ago, one superintendent was singled out by the media for the strong results in her district. Instead of resting on her laurels, this leader made a public statement that, in her view, the results were not yet good enough. The evidence indicated that, while the overall graduation rate for Indigenous learners was almost at a par with their non-Indigenous peers, the participation rates in academic mathematics, science, and English courses lagged behind.

She wanted dignity, purpose, and genuine options for *every* learner in the district. This meant tackling the barriers and obstacles keeping Indigenous learners out of the kinds of courses that offered the strongest post-secondary options. It takes tough conversations to say that good is not really enough. Acknowledging the hard work underway that is leading to a better set of outcomes—and then being prepared to push on to create genuinely equitable outcomes for everyone—takes courage.

We know as educators that we can be really hard on ourselves. Many of us are always wondering what more can be done, whose needs aren't being met, what we can do better, and how we can be better. Sometimes enough really is enough—at least for a short while. Context matters a lot, and it is only through probing conversations at the Checking stage that your team can make this call.

STEP 4: TIME TO CELEBRATE!

Whether or not you have decided that you have made enough of a difference, it *is* important to acknowledge the differences you are making. Taking the time to celebrate the differences that *are* being made for learners is validating, respectful, and motivating. We hope you will learn to celebrate the genuine gains you are making while still holding onto and working hard toward your critically important equity goals.

A REMINDER ABOUT CHECKING:

Checking Is

- Knowing what you want to accomplish for your learners
- Revisiting the goals you set for your learners at the beginning of the Spiral and the questions you decided on in the Scanning stage
- Listening to your learners
- Setting the expectation that your actions will make a substantial difference for all learners

- Being open to new indicators of success
- Opening up new questions
- Sharing your findings with others

Checking Is Not

- A tick box to check off at the end of the process
- Being satisfied with some difference for some learners
- Conducted without learners being involved
- Justifying your actions
- Using data simply because it is easily accessible
- Acccpting assumptions without challenge

BIG IDEAS FROM CHAPTER 8

- Checking requires evaluative thinking as we gather, organize, and make sense of the evidence.
- The closer the evidence is to the learner, the more compelling it is for teachers.
- The two key questions are essential at the Scanning and Checking stages.
- When we deeply value equity goals, Checking means we ask hard questions about equity.
- New competencies require new indicators of success.
- Checking is a time to celebrate growth before rushing on.

FREQUENTLY ASKED QUESTIONS ABOUT CHECKING

Can we use the provincial (state, national) student learning surveys as evidence at the Checking stage?

Of course—with caution. Most large-scale surveys contain a great many questions and are designed to provide broad patterns and to point out areas for further investigation. You could carefully select three or four questions from these larger surveys that seem particularly relevant to your context and then use them to probe more deeply at both the Scanning and the Checking stages.

Our focus is on social-emotional learning (SEL). What can we use as evidence to see if our learners are getting stronger?

There are a lot of survey instruments available if you are looking at SEL, grit, perseverance, or growth mindset. A simple search online will reveal scores of resources and a myriad of programs. It can be daunting trying to select both the approach and the metrics that fit your context. One of the most comprehensive sources for SEL is the Collaborative for Academic, Social and Emotional Learning (CASEL) website.[24] Here you will find guidance for selecting and using a range of SEL assessment guides. Another strong resource is the Student Experience Research Network.[25] We also encourage schools to use their networks of contacts to find a school that has had this focus for several years and has created meaningful change as a result. Learning from colleagues who have "been there and done that" is often very motivating.

Keep in mind that you can only assess what you have taught and what you expect students to learn. Having access to a range of assessment options can give you some ideas of what evidence to look for. And the same advice we provided earlier about surveys holds true again here. Limit the questions to the specific areas on which you have focused. If you have been focused on building empathy, then you will be looking for evidence that your learners are able to see things from another point of view. If your focus has been on growth mindset, then you will be observing the strategies that your learners are able to apply when they hit an obstacle. The sharper your focus, the clearer you will be on the evidence to collect.

QUESTIONS FOR LEARNING CONVERSATIONS

1. What do you think about the concept of big data compared to small or street-level data? How can you encourage the use of "close-to-the-learner" sources of evidence in your school?
2. What sources of evidence will give your inquiry team the clearest idea of how much difference you are making—especially to those students who are currently most disadvantaged?
3. How will you involve your learners at the Checking stage?
4. Celebrating genuine gains matters. How and when will you celebrate the gains that you are collectively making?
5. As a result of your first experience with the Spiral, what advice would you give to other schools starting out?

LEADERSHIP MOVES

- Be very clear on the changes you want to make for your learners and the evidence that will be most helpful in determining the extent to which you are making a difference.
- Be curious about what is working and what isn't working—for what students and under what conditions. Model evaluative thinking and non-defensiveness.
- Be informed about indicators of school success that will help your staff ask tough questions about the data they have collected.
- Provide time for all staff to make meaning from the evidence collected. Don't rush the thinking.

9

SPIRALS ACROSS NETWORKS

Going Deeper and Going Further

KW Elementary School is located in a rural community that has faced a great deal of economic uncertainty and many challenges. The staff had worked with the Spiral for a few years, and they had seen steady growth in their focus areas of oral expression and reading comprehension. At the same time, as they reflected on the progress they were making, many staff commented on the increased stress and anxiety that seemed to be related to the pandemic. They were concerned about the growing number of learners who were displaying unkind words and actions toward peers and staff. As they started a new school year, they asked their students to describe what kindness looks like and what different forms kindness could take. Very few were able to provide thoughtful answers.

The staff dove into learning more about teaching empathy and decided to shift their focus to building kindness and empathy by providing their students with the chance to engage in intentional, purposeful, and practical acts of kindness. They called their co-designed initiative Build Grow Share. This new focus has led to substantial changes in students' understanding and actions. Their inquiry is also helping to create more positive connections within the community as a whole. Other network schools have expressed interest in learning from KW and are designing similar approaches. Their work is spiralling deeper and wider.

THE FIRST TIME through the Spiral gives inquiry teams a chance to understand the framework and to experience what can happen when you listen deeply to your learners. The real power of the Spiral comes as you work with it over time. If you persevere, by the second and third year you will have growing evidence that your learners are benefitting and your whole school learning culture is changing for the better. As you link your work with other schools, you can begin to sense that you are making a contribution to overall system change. In this final chapter, we'll share some ideas about depth and breadth, including the impact that can happen when schools come together in networks, large and small.

GOING DEEPER

Changing the experiences of Indigenous learners in our schools—and increasing knowledge and respect for Indigenous ways of knowing—is a major passion for us both. As we mentioned in the introduction, our professional lives changed in 2009 when Dr. Trish Rosborough asked us to support her work with the Aboriginal Education Branch at the Ministry of Education through a networking strategy. At that time, school districts had been encouraged to enter into agreements with local Indigenous communities to focus on enhancing the experiences of Indigenous learners. A lot of hard work went into these agreements, and yet the impact was not yet being seen in practice. At that meeting on a dark rainy day over a cup of coffee, Trish presented us with the challenge of engaging teachers and principals in realizing the goals of these agreements at the school and classroom levels.

Our answer was a resounding yes. We started by inviting network schools to get involved. At first the work was quite tentative. Most school teams initially chose to do something that they were familiar with and that didn't cause them too much discomfort. Their actions often revolved around using Indigenous-themed picture books as part of their literacy program. Teachers wanted students to learn more through these stories about the negative impact of colonization and the attempted destruction of Indigenous culture. We were concerned that schools might not move beyond the focus on literature. We were reminded of Debbie Leighton Stephens's advice: "If you aren't squirming, you aren't learning." We wondered if the network was creating enough space for teams to productively squirm.

Encouragingly, teams didn't stay stuck for long. By the second and third years, many schools began incorporating such Indigenous strategies as the circle check-in into their daily routines. Local Elders were leading classroom sessions, and many teachers began to move learning and teaching out of the school building and onto the land. Instead of a camping trip at the end of the year as a reward, teachers, with the support of local Indigenous leaders, were starting the year with outdoor experiences to build community and connection to the local territory.

As more time went by, school teams began to learn words and concepts from the local Indigenous language. They began to shift the visual identity of their schools to reflect the Indigenous culture of the territory. Teachers and cultural support workers became more comfortable and confident in teaching about the history of residential schools. They also focused on the many contributions of Indigenous peoples to current-day Canada. Indigenous understandings were starting to be infused into all curriculum areas. The leadership of strong Indigenous practitioners within the network became increasingly visible and valued.

Participants in school tours from other countries commented positively on the changes they were seeing and vowed to use what they learned in their own settings. As Laura, an educator from Australia, commented:

> Visiting Canada was a pivotal moment for me, both in terms of professional development and personal growth. The concept of "Truth before Reconciliation" is so simple, yet the way that it played out in each and every school and echoed in the voices of each student and educator we met made it so much more than just words. It wasn't long after returning home that we began to dig deeper into our

> own context and implement our own learning. I also really loved how students were outside in nature for so many of their lessons and had the opportunity to play in all kinds of weather. This has emboldened me to embrace the outdoors (not something that comes naturally) a lot more and find opportunities to connect our learning with outdoor spaces.[1]

While there is still a great deal of work to be done before we reach our goals of equity and quality for all learners, we are seeing an increasing number of schools that are open to new learning and that are willing to ask the hard questions demanded by the Spiral.

Early on in our work with the network, Debbie Leighton Stephens taught us the importance of the term Hagwil yaan (walk slowly) from the Sm'algya̱x language. Through listening to a personal story of dealing with a dangerous situation from Ts'msyen Elder Alex Campbell, Debbie learned that this teaching helps us to remember that "watching for the signs, paying close attention, and being present" really matters. Debbie continuously encourages us "to walk slowly, walk beside each other, and be the known face" as we deepen our inquiries and work together to combat racism.

Tsun Dax Laura Tait, another Ts'msyen educator and senior district leader in British Columbia (BC), has developed a framework to help all of us deepen Indigenous understandings as a network and as a system. The metaphor of paddling to deeper waters has helped all network members understand that decolonizing the system requires us to get started and to keep moving together. Appendix A reflects the stages of understanding and action that are necessary. Please consider this as a guide for reflection in your own setting.

Jo Chrona, another network leader with Ts'msyen ancestry, is the author of *Wayi Wah! Indigenous Pedagogies: An Act for Reconciliation and Anti-Racist Education* (in press 2022). She is teaching inquiry network schools to think about Indigenous understandings through the perspective of her evolving anti-racism framework. In a March 2021 blog post she explored the journey of anti-racism in this way:

> From some recent work in helping educators move into anti-racist thinking and acting in K-12 education in BC, especially with regards to anti-Indigenous racism, I have been thinking about the progressions we move through (linear and

cyclical) in our anti-racist understanding and doing. Below is an adaptation of the "Becoming Anti-Racist" graphic by Andrew M. Ibrahim, MD, MSc (based on previous work by Dr. Kendi). I have added ideas and extended the arrow to indicate continual learning and growth.[2]

We appreciate Jo Chrona's willingness to share her graphic with us, and we hope that the hard questions demanded by the Spiral of Inquiry will help us all move along the continuum to a place of continuous learning and growth, activism, and advocacy.

Figure 9.1. Becoming Anti-Racist

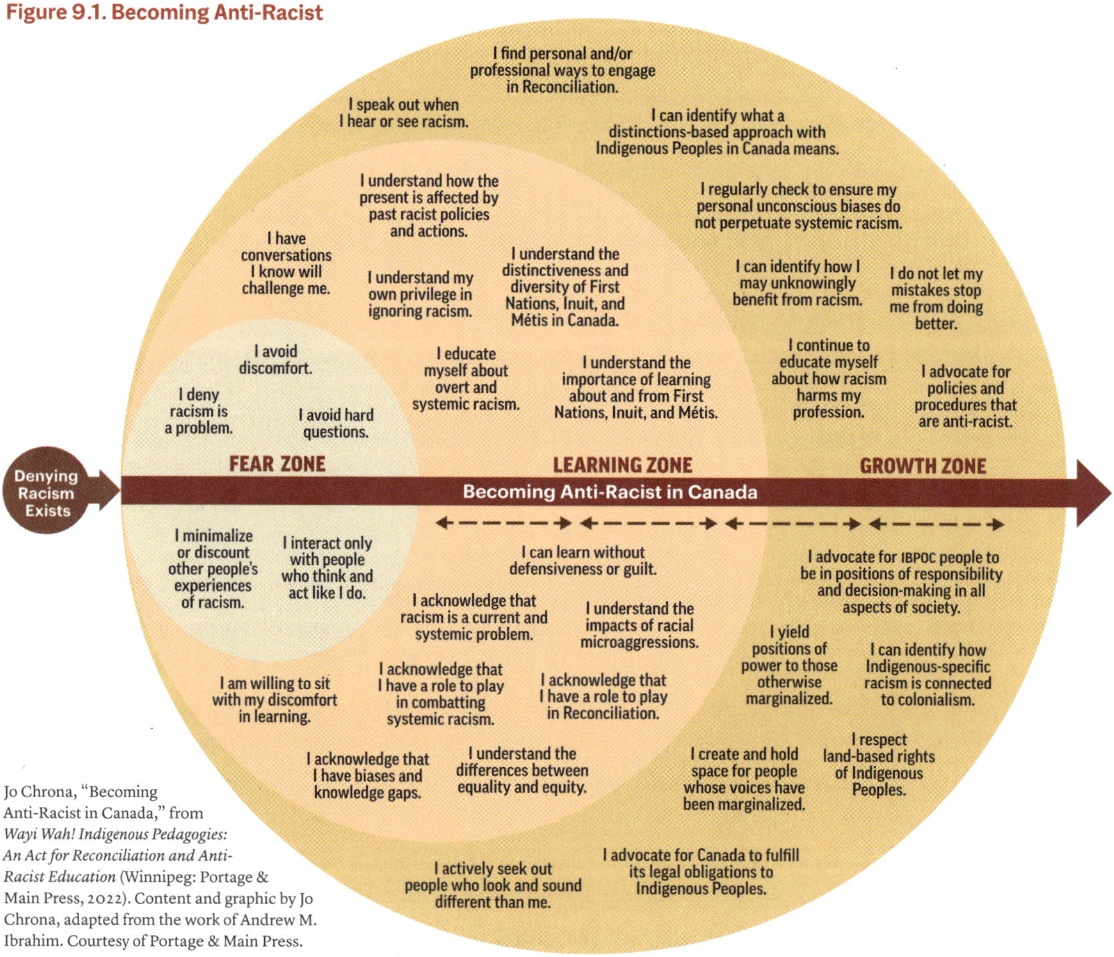

Jo Chrona, "Becoming Anti-Racist in Canada," from *Wayi Wah! Indigenous Pedagogies: An Act for Reconciliation and Anti-Racist Education* (Winnipeg: Portage & Main Press, 2022). Content and graphic by Jo Chrona, adapted from the work of Andrew M. Ibrahim. Courtesy of Portage & Main Press.

Journeying as learning. Since 2018, there have been groups of schools in BC focused on improving transitions for Indigenous learners. Jana Maatoyokom Fox, a district leader with Blackfoot and Navajo heritage, has been co-leading this study with Lori Burger. Twenty-eight middle and secondary schools are part of the third cohort that was launched in the fall of 2021.[3] We invited Jana Maatoyokom Fox to share the ways in which she sees the connections between the Spiral of Inquiry and Indigenous ways of knowing:

> *Journeying as learning* is a mindset shared by many cultural groups. This is a concept I've repeatedly encountered in my own learning from Indigenous knowledge holders, scholars, and colleagues. Through story, literature, example, and experience, they have taught me that we are all on a lifelong journey of *coming to know*. Mi'kmaw scholar, knowledge keeper, and educator, Marie Battiste (2013), shares teachings about lifelong learning from Saulteaux Elder Danny Musqua: "Each of us has a journey on earth that is solely about learning ... learning is the purpose of our life journey" (p. 18).[4]

Key for us is the understanding that the Spiral is never-ending. We appreciated the insight from Alex, the 8-year-old learner whom we quoted in chapter 7, when he wrote, "Spirals never stop, just like my learning never stops." The Spiral of Inquiry is a process for professional learning to change outcomes for learners, and as we work with it over time, it becomes an enduring way of being. Jana Maatoyokom Fox goes on to say:

> The moral purpose and inclusive, relational, and process-oriented nature of the Networks of Inquiry and Indigenous Education (NOIIE) and the Spiral of Inquiry cultivates an environment that brings multiple stories together, weaving a pathway for like-minded, curious educators to explore. When we engage in the Spiral of Inquiry, we work as a collective: an interdependent network of educators interconnected and nested within the complex organizational layers of the education system.
>
> I believe, from an Indigenous lens, we find strength and continue our journey in challenging times when we have constructed a pathway of stories and knowledge, and we believe in the process and the framework to carry us through.

> Acknowledging the unfamiliar, our assumptions, our biases, and our own fixed mindsets is inherently embedded within the phases of the Spiral of Inquiry. So too is reflecting on our learning, our actions, and the shifts in our thinking that help move us to a new familiar. These are also fundamental behaviours of a life-long learner.[5]

One of the First Peoples Principles of Learning is that "Learning is holistic, reflexive, reflective, experiential, and relational (focused on connectedness, reciprocal relationships, and a sense of place)."[6] Catherine McGregor, the researcher studying NOIIE, has introduced the phrase "catalytic affiliation"[7] to describe how connecting through networks has an animating effect on deepening and spreading the impact of thoughtful work in schools. When trusting relationships build over time, strong practices can travel faster and further.

GOING FURTHER THROUGH STUDENT LEADERSHIP

In chapter 2 we introduced you to three groups of student leaders at a suburban secondary school who used the Spiral of Inquiry and the decision-making framework to tackle loneliness, cyberbullying, and racism. The group working on cyberbullying reached out to Harvard researchers Carrie James and Emily Weinstein, co-authors of *Teaching Digital Citizens in Today's World*. Those researchers formed a productive learning partnership with these bold youth leaders.

The work on anti-racism spread by word of mouth to the other secondary schools in the district, and new groups of student leaders applied the Spiral to anti-racism work in their own schools. The provincial Ministry of Multiculturalism got wind of this initiative and provided the district with a grant to create a video to show other student groups how they might collaborate to create anti-racist school cultures.

At the same time, the Grades 6–7 teaching team at a partner elementary school became aware of this student leadership work. These teachers decided that they would apply the decision-making framework to a community-service initiative. Small groups of learners identified a specific community need and generated ways to make a positive contribution in partnership with community members. They then partnered with the local newspaper[8] to publish stories about their learning.

According to the newspaper's article on this project, when students were faced with the question, "What action can I take that would positively impact someone or something in my community?" they considered what was truly important to them and then developed a plan. Their teacher told the reporter that these students researched agencies such as the food bank and the animal shelter to see what ways they could get involved, and came up with three possible options. They then carefully measured each option against the criteria for the project. As the teacher also explained, the project needed to be "closely related to our values, have a minimal cost, be COVID-19-friendly, [be] able to measure impact in some way, and [be] an achievable plan." These criteria "helped them narrow down [the options] to their best choice."[9]

These young leaders communicated with local agencies, teachers, and family members to acquire the support they needed to realize their plans. As these students move on to high school they will bring this decision-making knowledge and action-oriented stance to their larger setting. These are citizens on the move.

The power of three

In architecture, the triangle is considered a particularly strong shape because it has a strong base and a strong support. In social network theory, the Latin term *tertius iungens* refers to a strategic way of bringing together individuals. Scholars Michael Kent, Erich J. Sommerfeldt, and Adam J. Saffer suggest that the concept of *tertius iungens* reflects the good that occurs when a third person creates a link between two previously disconnected individuals.[10] We have seen this power of three play out in a number of ways as schools in groups of three work together as small networks.

An early example, which we sometimes refer to as the trilogy, involved three small schools in a northern BC community. Teachers and principals from these schools decided to work together on their inquiries when they realized that they had identified similar focus areas. They began engaging in professional learning together on a monthly basis. They didn't have access to a lot of money for their professional learning work but found that they could go further by pooling the funding they *did* have as a trio of schools.

Over a few years of working skillfully together, they were able to have a significant impact on the learners they served, and their work became known and adopted provincially. In describing the power of their teamwork, they insisted that ordering Chinese food and ending their planning meetings in a hot tub in the middle of winter were key parts of their process. We weren't so sure about the hot tub, but we were intrigued by their spirited approach and impressed by the learning gains for their students.

GOING FURTHER TOGETHER GLOBALLY

In their book, *Spirit Work and the Science of Collaboration*, Michael Fullan and Mark Edwards state:

> Experiences of true collaboration are always identical, no matter your age or cultural background. We feel connected, energized, empowered, inspired, creative, and purposeful. Together we just want to get the work done, the problem solved. Looking back on these experiences, we recall the joy we felt at being together, giving it our best, persevering.[11]

This statement reflects the sense of satisfaction and connection that we are experiencing as part of an expanding global network. In her foreword to *Spirit Work*, Margaret Wheatley writes, "We believe that the human spirit has a tendency to join with others to solve the deepest problems."[12]

We appreciate the proverb, "If you want to go fast, go alone; if you want to go far, go together." We are learning a great deal from the inquiry networks that are growing around the world. What these educator-led networks have in common is the commitment to applying the Spiral of Inquiry to reach for greater equity and quality in their schools and systems. These network leaders share a spirit of generosity by making their work public, by sharing resources with each other, and by hosting tours. They also make their learning visible through publications, through their participation in various network symposia, and through presentations at international conferences.

We have the greatest respect for the educators who have stepped up to lead this work, and we offer the following examples to illustrate the ways in which networks are evolving and learning from each other.

British Columbia, the Yukon, and Manitoba

The Canadian educators in BC, the Yukon, and Manitoba who lead regional and local networks are a very special group. Without exception, they are reflective and action-oriented practitioners who are determined to make as much of a difference as they possibly can. They are genuinely interested in a wide range of perspectives and are willing to work hard to create change on the ground in their own settings and in the larger arena of the province or territory. Their professional roles vary from classroom teacher to district superintendent, and they subscribe to the network norm that encourages leaders to "Leave your formal role at the door and enter as a learner." In addition to helping create a strategic direction for the network, they are involved in coaching school inquiry teams, planning and hosting symposia, participating in research studies, coordinating regional meetings, and providing wisdom and guidance as we learn more about Indigenous ways of knowing.

Observing the work of these leaders continually inspires us and reinforces our determination to create the conditions for the kind of leadership that strengthens the fabric of our democracy. The Spiral process is one way to make sure that influence is widely shared and that fair processes for determining a direction are part of the culture of a school. Julie Battilana and Tizana Casciaro stress the importance of such a process in "It's Up to Us," the final chapter of their book *Power, for All: How it Really Works and Why It Is Everyone's Business*:

> We can counteract the concentration of power by increasing our collective ability to deliberate, discuss, and decide on the rules of the game in our workplaces and more broadly in society. This is where democracy comes into play. Without the ability to participate as equals in democratic systems, we throw away the ability to decide our futures together.[13]

As the BC-Yukon-Manitoba network has grown and evolved, so too have the ways in which the network leaders contribute to a stronger and more equitable learning system. It is deeply encouraging for us to see many network leaders now enrolled in graduate and doctoral programs, leading teacher preparation programs, teaching university courses, maintaining an active presence on social media, and publishing articles and books.

New South Wales

Our connection with Australia began with our serendipitous meeting with two principals in Sydney. Over the past decade we have visited the schools led by Natalie Mansour and David Martin many times, and we have been pleased to host them as they have brought a number of study tours to BC. The links between our networks have led to BC educators, parents, and students presenting at the New South Wales (NSW) Network of Inquiry and Innovation (NOII) gatherings as well as NSW teams sharing their expertise at learning events in BC. The exchange of the professional learning practices in our two settings has been mutually advantageous.

We learned about the power of "early-career residentials" as a professional learning structure from these Australian leaders.[14] At the early-career residential, all teachers new to their schools spend an evening and a day in a beautiful retreat setting over the weekend. They share a meal and begin to form community. Next, they spend time diving into new professional learning on topics such as critical thinking strategies and formative assessment. When the new teachers return to their schools the following week, they are supported by their more experienced teaching colleagues in trying out new strategies. This relationship-building approach has since been adapted and applied in a number of settings. Their work is having a big impact—in and beyond the borders of their state.

Queensland and the Northern Territory

In Queensland the inquiry network is led by a trio of elementary educators, all of whom are experienced school principals. David Turner, Zoe Elder, and Vicki Baker are doing exceptional work in building a networked community focused on student agency and powerful thinking routines. David, as a director of professional learning, has led many international tours, including to BC and the Yukon.

The Queensland team welcomed five principals from Darwin to join them at an early symposium in 2016. This team, led by Robyn Thorpe and Jackie Roberts, then wrote a proposal to their Northern Territory Department of Education to start a local inquiry network. With some initial financial support from the Department, NOII NT was launched. Some of the NT team have visited BC and the Yukon, and others have participated in the annual NOII NSW symposium. Teacher-leaders and principals from the Sydney schools have travelled to Darwin for their gatherings. The links continue to grow.

Aotearoa/New Zealand

There is a powerful collaboration taking place in Aotearoa/New Zealand with schools that work with Rebbecca Sweeney and CORE Education, a professional development organization with national influence. Rebbecca Sweeney uses her strong inquiry skills and her coaching experience to help schools deepen their professional learning work through the Spiral of Inquiry. She has observed that "human minds are wired to connect and this is as important for adult learners as it is for young learners in schools."[15] The Spiral of Inquiry, along with Story Hui,[16] a strong visual storytelling methodology, encourages dialogue between team members and supports ongoing connections between teachers and learners.

England

Several years ago, we were introduced to Whole Education (WE) in England, a "dynamic network of schools and partners who are united in their belief that all children and young people deserve a fully rounded education."[17] Within WE, there is a growing network of schools that apply the Spiral of Inquiry to address significant challenges of equity and quality, including focusing on the needs of some of the most vulnerable learners—those with special education needs and those in danger of being excluded.[18]

Educators from WE have participated in study tours to BC and have had a powerful influence on the ways in which coaching support is now provided in our province. We have appreciated working with the leaders of the Spirals initiative at WE, and we have learned a great deal from our conversations with the Executive Director, Douglas Archibald. In the early days of the Spirals work within WE, Louise Stoll and Julie Temperley conducted a review of the impact of Spirals after the first year of its use. This report has influenced work in other parts of the global network. The generosity of the WE team in welcoming educators from Sweden and Barcelona has helped to build more global links.

Sweden

A study tour from Sweden to a school district in BC a few years ago led to curiosity about the potential for an inquiry network in that country and an invitation from WE to attend a Spirals launch in London. Two exceptional educators and experienced principals, Lillemor Rehnberg and Ingela Netz, now lead an innovative national program that uses the Spiral of Inquiry as the basis for principal leadership development. Small networks within Sweden are now forming. Rehnberg and Netz view themselves "as 'connectors' who have a broad overview of the Spiral framework and who organize meetings with the intent of promoting a generous sharing of knowledge and experiences from all levels of the school system, both nationally and internationally."[19]

Networks in other countries are learning a great deal from Swedish educators. One of the take-aways is the adoption of *fika*, a practice we are now building into all network meetings. On the surface fika might be viewed as an extended coffee break; however, we have learned from Swedish colleagues how important it is to make time to stop and socialize, to take a pause, to refresh our brains and to strengthen relationships. This is the true meaning of fika. The Spiral asks you to slow down the urge for immediate action in order to make sure the actions you do take are well considered and informed. Fika reminds us again of the importance of slowing down and focusing on relationships.

Barcelona and Madrid

The history of the development of networks of inquiry in Spain, which began in Barcelona and now attract interest across the country, is intriguing. In 2016, Begonya Folch Martinez was working with an initiative called Escola Nova 21 on school transformation.

She and the Escola Nova team connected with David Istance (the lead researcher on the Innovative Learning Environment Study at the Centre for Educational Research and Innovation [CERI] at the OECD) for advice. From him they learned about the Spirals of Inquiry and the inquiry networks in BC. With the support of the Jaume Bofill Foundation, the Spiral of Inquiry was introduced to five hundred schools in the Catalan region.

The next step was taken in 2020 when the La Caixa foundation, with the leadership of Núria Vives Font, supported a pilot program involving ten schools in Madrid. Begonya Folch Martinez and her colleague Victoria Ibañez Gonzalez supported this initiative in a time of considerable challenge as the pandemic prevented in-person meetings. Nevertheless, the work that is underway is impressive. This team is creating a culture of inquiry in a growing number of schools.

WHAT IS NEXT?

When we began this work over two decades ago, we didn't anticipate the impact it would have. Nor did we imagine that we would be even more passionate about our commitment to the idea of a network than when we started. And we are encouraged to see interest in the network model continue to spread. There is now an emerging network in Wales focused on well-being and some highly promising work within the state of Hawaii focused on strengthening school identity and learner confidence. Recently we have been invited to share some ideas about networks and the Spiral of Inquiry with new colleagues in Latvia. Who knows what might be next?

The image we chose for the "About Us" page of the NOIIE website[20] came from the work of New Zealand environmental photographer Martin Hill. He gave us permission to use his image of floating stones to symbolize the inquiry network.[21] Two things struck us about this image when we first saw it on a card in a local store. The first is that it is very rare (at least in our experience) to see stones that float. The second is that the ripples that emanate from the stones seem to have no end point.

At the time, we were reading *Confidence* by Rosabeth Moss Kanter. *Confidence* teaches that leadership is not about walking on water. It is about creating the conditions so that others can.[22] This has been part of our vision for the network—creating the conditions so that others can do their finest work.

We believe that inquiry leadership teams are making a genuine contribution to the strengthening of the practices of participatory democracy at the school and community levels. Recent ideas from Daniel Kahneman, Olivier Sibony, and Cass R. Sunstein about how destructive "noise" can be in our decision-making processes have made us realize that we need to be proactive in all our organizations.[23] We need to practise and model how we want our learners—and our policy-makers—to be. Getting better at making decisions about how to change our school by listening to learners, by listening to families and community members, and by listening to each other in respectful ways really matters.

We need to follow the advice of the Elders who say that the great Creator gave us two ears and one mouth so that we can listen more than we talk. Noise leads to poor decisions because it warps the process when the loudest and least informed voices speak first in meetings. Good frameworks, norms, and strategies can change this. We want schools, as public institutions, to model the way forward. We want the voices of learners to count. We want to support meaningful youth leadership that is focused on living well with one another and in harmony with nature.

Over the next decade the decisions we make about how we are all going to live together in a sustainable way will be critically important. In many places youth and school staffs are already taking the lead in the vital work of environmental stewardship. Our planet needs all of us to work together to honour and protect the natural world. Schools can play a key role in the essential work of building trust and arriving at reconciliation with Indigenous peoples.

At the beginning of this book we expressed our desire to help create schools as places where hope is nurtured, options are expanded, and positive futures are created. We believe that developing lifelong curiosity in adults and young people is critically important. The Spiral of Inquiry is designed to build curiosity and to change the experiences of learners. When whole systems embrace inquiry-mindedness as a professional way of life we will be well on our way to making sure that *every* learner walks the stage with dignity, purpose, and options.

BIG IDEAS FROM CHAPTER 9

- The more experienced you and your team become with the Spiral of Inquiry, the deeper your work will become.
- Discomfort is often a key aspect of deep learning.
- Connecting with other schools in small and big networks sustains momentum and increases impact.
- Network leadership matters. Think of leadership as creating conditions for others to succeed. This does not depend exclusively on role.
- The Spiral of Inquiry is a never-ending process.

FREQUENTLY ASKED QUESTIONS

How do I start a network?

We have learned that networks cannot be controlled, managed, or directed. They can be encouraged, supported, and led. We have also learned the importance of voluntary network participation, an invitational stance, and finding ways to say thank-you. Our networks don't operate with a lot of money. In most cases those leading the networks have regular full-time jobs and are doing this work out of a desire to contribute to the greater good. Acknowledging schools for making their work public through the publication of their case studies or through inviting them to participate in other sharing events is really important. The best starting point is to find a few like-minded colleagues, reach out for support, keep it simple, and just get going.

Where can I learn more?

Throughout the book we have included links to resources and organizations that we have found helpful. Don't hesitate to reach out through websites, Facebook, Twitter, or Instagram to other network leaders. A spirit of generosity is one of the important values of the inquiry networks. We learned from Indigenous Elders that we increase our influence by what we freely give away. Having said this, we also have a network ethic that if you learn something from another educator, school, network, or system, you will always acknowledge the source.

QUESTIONS FOR LEARNING CONVERSATIONS

1. In what ways will you encourage your teams to go deeper the second time through the Spiral?
2. How will you share your stories of impact?
3. In what ways do you see your school contributing to broader system change?
4. What does the term *catalytic affiliation* mean to you?
5. How will your inquiry work contribute to greater equity and quality for all learners?

LEADERSHIP MOVES

- Connect with two other schools. Consider forming a small network. Combine your resources. Set a hard, shared goal.
- Learn more about Indigenous perspectives, especially about sustainability and generosity.
- Think about how you could link your local network with other networks globally. There is much to learn from different contexts.
- Laugh often. Friendship and humour can sustain you through the tough times.

ACKNOWLEDGMENTS

WE WOULD LIKE to start by thanking every teacher, cultural support worker, vice-principal, principal, and district staff educator who is working or has worked in a network school. Your commitment to inquiry and to sharing your stories is helping to create a culture of professional curiosity. Collectively your work is making a big difference for tens of thousands of learners.

There is a key group of educators in British Columbia who serve as leaders in the Networks of Inquiry and Indigenous Education (NOIIE). In addition to helping create a strategic direction for the network, they are involved in coaching school inquiry teams, planning and hosting symposia, participating in research studies, coordinating regional meetings, providing wisdom and guidance as we learn more about Indigenous ways of knowing, leading school tours, writing articles, organizing and hosting online learning events, creating new publications, teaching undergraduate and graduate courses—and being ready to say "Yes" whenever asked.

A very special thank you to Jody Billingsley, Emma Burger, Jo Chrona, Andrea Davidson, Nicole Davey, Roberta Edzerza, Rosa Fazio, Paige Fisher, Jana Fox, Barb Hamblett, Michelle Iacobucci, Nancy Gordon, Tashi Kirincic, Debbie Koehn, Debbie Leighton-Stephens, Catherine Ludwig, Joanna Macintosh, Michelle Miller-Gauthier, Brooke Moore, Mia Moutray, Angela Stott, Laura Tait, Terry Taylor, and Heidi Wood.

Lynne Tomlinson has been with the network since the very first meeting in 1999. In everything she does, Lynne demonstrates a powerful commitment to equity, quality, and social justice. We are grateful for her friendship, her leadership, and her unflagging support. Donna Weaving's contributions during the first twenty years of the network helped keep us all grounded and connected. Sarah Lockman has always believed in the power of the network, and she continues to make everything better for all of us connected with NOIIE.

The growth of the network outside of British Columbia is taking place because of the vision and passion of inquiry-minded educators across the world. The leadership of Nicole Morgan in the Yukon is deeply appreciated, as is the leadership of Jen Donachuk in Manitoba. Globally our thanks go to Douglas Archibald, Vicki Baker, Hallie Baxter, Gemma Burns, Verity Cane, Jo Corrigan, Victoria Ibanez Gonzalez, Natalie Horrobin, Pua Kaai, Rosie Leonard Kane, Kim Le Bas, Natalie Mansour, Begonya Folch Martinez, David Martin, Ingela Netz, Michael Newcombe, Natasa Pantelic, Erin Ranie, Lillemor Rehnberg, Jackie Roberts, Britany Roestenburg, Sue Sessions, Anne Sliwa, Zoe Smith, Rebbecca Sweeney, Robyn Thorpe, and David Turner. We appreciate your belief in the power of the Spiral to transform learning and to create more equitable systems.

From the international community, we have especially benefitted from the research and advice of our colleagues and friends Lorna Earl, Valerie Hannon, David Istance, Tony Mackay, Amelia Peterson, Louise Stoll, and Helen Timperley. Each of you has made a contribution to our thinking and to our work. We are grateful to Louise Stoll for her research on schools as learning organizations and for her understanding of the potential of networks to create lasting change. We have also benefited from Louise's advice and keen attention to detail as we worked to shape our writing into this book.

Lorna Earl's generosity in introducing us to Helen Timperley and then organizing a retreat for the four of us in Colorado was instrumental in shaping the Spirals of Inquiry process. Helen Timperley and her colleagues at the University of Auckland continue to be powerful influences on our thinking. We value the body of professional learning research that Helen has created, and we really enjoyed the process of creating the Spirals model with her. Valerie Hannon has always productively provoked our thinking about innovation and systems. Amelia Peterson is an ongoing friend to the network and has provided an informed and lively voice at NOIIE symposia. David Istance's work with the innovative learning environments initiative continues to influence our leadership thinking. Tony Mackay's friendship, connections, encouragement, and drive have enriched our lives.

Over the last two decades we have had the chance to learn more about Indigenous understandings and worldviews. We are deeply grateful for this learning. Thanks to Joanne Archibald, Denise Augustine, Lori Burger, Jo Chrona, Debbie Leighton-Stephens, Jana Fox, Leona Prince, Trish Rosborough, Laura Tait, Lorna Wanosts'a7 Williams, and Heidi Wood for your wisdom and your friendship.

Our colleagues at the University of British Columbia have inspired our thinking and provided us with opportunities to learn, grow, and connect. Thank you to Deborah Butler, Nancy Perry, and Leyton Schnellert for your leadership in self-regulating learning. We are indebted to Kimberley Schonert-Reichl for her research on social-emotional learning. Wendy Carr and Blye Frank have provided encouragement and support every step of the way at UBC.

Catherine McGregor at the University of Victoria has been a friend to the network for many years. Her evaluation of the initial work of the Aboriginal Enhancement Schools Network and her review of the impact of the transitions work with the NOIIE have helped deepen and extend the thinking of all network schools. We are confident that her developing ideas about catalytic affiliation will further stretch thinking about the power and potential of inquiry networks.

At one point in our teaching careers we both taught English, so we know a lot about the power of feedback. Joanne Wise and Kathy Kaulbach were instrumental in clarifying our writing and illustrating our thinking when we produced *The Spiral Playbook* in 2017. We continue to enjoy our collaboration with Joanne and Kathy. Lesley Peterson at Portage & Main Press has provided invaluable editorial commentary and assistance throughout the final stages of this book.

Finally we would like to thank our friends and families for their patience, encouragement, and understanding. To Kate and Danielle—thanks for your ongoing support. To Frances and Sam—thanks for your enjoyment of learning and your sense of social justice. To Nora and Jack—thank you for reminding us of the importance of stories, curiosity, and play.

APPENDIX A

Indigenous Understandings Learning Progression – Nanaimo Ladysmith Public Schools

	Moving Toward the Water	Boarding the Canoe
	AWARENESS	**DEVELOPING**
	Implies a sense of "I need to know"	Implies my willingness to address my knowledge and beliefs
My beliefs and attitudes towards Indigenous peoples in Canada	• I recognize that my knowledge may need to be enhanced. • I am aware that issues exist around reconciling with Indigenous peoples. • I am aware that Canada has a need for reconciliation and historical truth from an Indigenous perspective.	• I am demonstrating a willingness t enhance my knowledge. • I may bring an informed perspecti to current issues. • I recognize my own cultural beliefs and values. • I recognize the existence of my bia and privilege.
My knowledge and understanding of Indigenous peoples and history on local, regional, and national levels in Canada	• Indigenous peoples and territories • Indigenous languages and cultures • Indigenous worldviews • Canadian history as it pertains to Indigenous peoples' history and current issues • Some of Canada's inaccurate portrayals of history	• Indigenous peoples and territories including whose land I'm on • Indigenous languages and cultures including my local context • Indigenous worldview • Impact of colonization and policies on present-day Indigenous people • Contributions of Indigenous peopl to contemporary society

Laura Tait, Nanaimo Ladysmith Public Schools, 2011, 2012, 2017, 2019. Used with permission.

Raising Your Paddle	Journey Into Deeper Waters
ACQUIRING	**ACTION/ADVOCACY**
Implies a demonstration of my understanding and respect	Implies a demonstration of my respect and commitment to advocacy
I demonstrate a responsibility to enhance my knowledge and understanding. I possess an intention to bring an informed and critical perspective to current issues and I act upon that intention. I demonstrate respect for Indigenous people. I have an understanding of how my bias and privilege impacts marginalized populations ("others"). My beliefs and values are transparent and supportive to the success of all	• I provide leadership to enhance others' knowledge and understanding. • I seek out opportunities to act on injustices toward Indigenous people. • My informed understanding is impacting systems and structures. • I am actively advocating for systemic changes.
Indigenous peoples and territories Indigenous languages and cultures The language born from the land where I live Indigenous worldview including interconnectedness of all living beings History and the impact of colonization Impact of the Indian Act on present-day Indigenous people Contributions of Indigenous people to contemporary society	• Impact of the dominant culture, while striving to foster an Indigenous worldview • Embedding knowledge and respect for Indigenous pedagogy in practices • Land and environmental stewardship • Elevating Indigenous voices and protecting Indigenous ways of life

NOTES

INTRODUCTION

1 Formal leader refers to principals, vice-principals, head teachers, department heads—anyone with authority and special responsibilities.

2 The Network of Performance Based Schools and the Aboriginal Enhancement Schools Network formally became the Networks of Inquiry and Indigenous Education (NOIIE) in 2016. See "The Networks."

3 First Nations Education Steering Committee, "First Peoples Principles."

4 Winthrop, Barton, and McGivney, *Leapfrogging Inequality*, 9.

5 "Common Hopi Symbols," AAANativeArts.com, https://www.aaanativearts.com/hopi-symbols.

6 First Nations Education Steering Committee, "First Peoples Principles."

7 See "Truth and Reconciliation Commission of Canada," National Centre for Truth and Reconciliation, University of Manitoba, 2021, https://nctr.ca/about/history-of-the-trc/truth-and-reconciliation-commission-of-canada/.

8 Leona Prince, "Spirals of Inquiry: A Tool for Reconciliation," Presentation at International Conference for School Effectiveness and Improvement (ICSEI), Virtual Conference, March 8, 2021, https://youtu.be/O02mbR0U94Q.

CHAPTER 1

1 We use the word *educator* as an inclusive term to reflect anyone (teacher, support worker, cultural worker, educational assistant, principal) in the school community who works directly with young people.

2 Simon Sinek, "How Great Leaders Inspire Action," TEDx Talks, May 4, 2010, https://www.ted.com/talks/simon_sinek_how_great_leaders_inspire_action/transcript?language=en.

3 Murphy, "HARD Goals, Not SMART Goals."

4 Watkins, Peterson, and Mehta, "Transforming School Districts," 3 (original emphasis).

5 Mehta and Fine, *In Search of Deeper Learning*, 76.

6 Goodwin, *Building a Curious School*, 6.

7 Engel, *Hungry Mind*, 77.

8 Engel, 81.

9 Engel, 81.

10 EL Education, 2022, https://eleducation.org/. On the related concept of "compassionate curiosity," see also Amanda Morin, "How to Show Empathy to Your Students With Compassionate Curiosity," Understood, understood.org/en/articles/using-compassionate-curiosity-to-drive-empathy.

11 Dweck, *New Psychology*, 238 (original emphasis).

12 Boaler, *Limitless Mind*, 13.

13 Boaler, 13.

14 Boaler, 45.

15 Boaler, 77.

16 Boaler, 101.

17 Boaler, 134.

18 Boaler, 166.

19 Fryberg, Covarrubias, and Burack, "Ongoing Psychological Colonization," 119.

20 Jensen et al., *Beyond PD*, 5.

21 See Istance and Dumont, "Future Directions."

CHAPTER 2

1 "Middle Years Development Instrument," Human Early Learning Partnership, http://earlylearning.ubc.ca/mdi/.

2 Walsh, "Science of Resilience."

3 The 2 x 10 strategy was first described and researched by Raymond J. Wlodkowski in *Motivational Opportunities for Successful Teaching: Leader's Guide* (Phoenix, AZ: Universal Dimensions, 1983).

4 Hattie and Timperley, "Power of Feedback," 88–90.

5 Dumont, Istance, and Benavides, eds., *The Nature of Learning.*

6 Jo Chrona, "Background of FPPL and Current Contexts," *First Peoples Principles of Learning* (blog), 2014, updated 2015, updated April 2016, https://firstpeoplesprinciplesoflearning.wordpress.com.

7 Robert [pseud.], email to authors, 2021.

8 "About Universal Design for Learning," CAST, 2022, https://www.cast.org/impact/universal-design-for-learning-udl.

9 Deb [pseud.], email to authors, 2021.

10 Personal conversation with authors at a Spirals session in Gavle, Sweden, March 5, 2018.

11 Network leader, personal conversation with authors at NOIIE symposium, May 2017.

CHAPTER 3

1 Timperley, comment to participants, NOIIE Symposium: Doing What Matters Most, Vancouver, May 10–11, 2019.

2 Le Fevre et al., *Leading Powerful Professional Learning*, 58–66.

3 For a brief overview of the two systems, see Kahneman, *Thinking, Fast and Slow*, 20–24.

4 Failing et al., *Decision Playbook*, 12.

5 Failing et al., 15.

6 Timperley et al., *Leading Professional Learning*, 69.

CHAPTER 4

1 Leyton Schnellert, comment to participants, presentation by Schnellert, Mehiabeen Datoo, Donn Kozak, and Miriam Miller, "How Professional Learning Networks Spark and Sustain Innovation," International Congress for School Effectiveness and Improvement (ICSEI), Virtual Congress, January 10, 2022.

2 Bishop et al., *Te Kōtahitanga*, 27–33.

3 One resource this school found especially helpful was Gail Boushey and Joan Moser, *The Daily 5: Fostering Literacy Independence in the Elementary Grades* (Portsmouth, NH: Stenhouse, 2014).

4 Grant, *Think Again*, 4.

5 Grant, 2.

6 Dalton, *Learning Talk*, 15.

7 Daly and Stoll, "Looking Back and Moving Forward," 206.

8 Daly and Stoll, 209.

9 Nottingham and Larsson, *Challenging Mindset*, 124.

10 Becki Larsen and Tori Silver, "Evelyn Dickson Elementary School, SD 91 Nechako Lakes," *Case Studies, NOIIE*, 2016, https://www.noiie.ca (article no longer available).

11 Timperley et al., *Leading Professional Learning*, 62.

12 Brown, *Daring Greatly*, 2.

CHAPTER 5

1 First Nations Education Steering Committee, "First Peoples Principles."

2 "Sesame Street: Ernie Learns to Put Down the Duckie," *Sesame Street*, July 17, 2009. 5:14. https://www.youtube.com/watch?v=acBixR_JRuM.

3 For a short description of the work of Dr. Williams, see Joel Barde, "Lil̓wat Nation Member Awarded Order of Canada," *Pique Newsmagazine*, January 12, 2020, https://www.piquenewsmagazine.com/sea-to-skylilwat-nation-member-awarded-order-of-canada-2509217.

4 Williams, "Ti wa7 szwatenem. What We Know," 38–39. To hear the Lil̓wat words and learn how to pronounce them, see Lorna Williams's website, Principles and Pronunciation Guide, https://sites.google.com/site/lulwatprinciples/home.

5 A small community in the Yukon Territory of northern Canada.

6 "Adapting to the Times: Committed to the Cause: Covid Response," Young 1ove, https://www.young1ove.org/covid-19response.

7 Angrist, Bergman, and Matsheng, "School's Out: Experimental Evidence," 5.

8 Lyfta, https://www.lyfta.com.

9 Everybody Deserves a Smile (EDAS), https://edas.ca.

10 Hargreaves and Shirley, *Well-Being in Schools*, xii.

11 Hargreaves and Shirley, 80.

12 For a good summary of this topic, see Boekaerts, "Crucial Role of Motivation."

13 See, for example, Valiente, Swanson, and Eisenberg, "Linking Students' Emotions."

14 For more information on this model, see "Learning in Depth Program," Simon Fraser University, Centre for Imaginative Education in the Faculty of Education, 2018, http://ierg.ca/LID/.

15 For more information on the transition work in BC, see "Indigenous Education."

16 Tilleczek, "Building Bridges," 68.

17 OECD, "Future of Education and Skills," 1.

18 Healey and Stroman, "Structures for Belonging," 2.

19 Healey and Stroman, 1.

20 Cited in Fullan, *Stratosphere*, 20.

21 See "Berry Street Education Model," Berry Street, https://www.berrystreet.org.au/what-we-do/education-services/berry-street-education-model.

22 A good place to start is the "Social and Emotional Learning Resource Finder," Faculty of Education, University of British Columbia, https://www.selresources.com.

23 See Ludwig, *Learning Tour Study Guide*.

24 From 2011 to 2016 we taught in the Master of Educational Leadership Program at Vancouver Island University. Since 2016 we have led the Transformative Educational Leadership Program (TELP) at the University of British Columbia.

25 Wiliam and Leahy, *Embedding Formative Assessment*, 2.

26 See Willowbank School, https://www.willowbank.school.nz.

27 Butler, Schnellert, and Perry, *Developing Self-Regulating Learners*, 183.

28 Butler, Schnellert, and Perry, 183.

29 Butler, Schnellert, and Perry, 130–33.

30 Butler, Schnellert, and Perry, 97–100.

31 Butler, Schnellert, and Perry, 115–16.

32 Butler, Schnellert, and Perry, 116–17.

33 Butler, Schnellert, and Perry, 113, 117–18.

34 For more information, see EL Education, https://eleducation.org.

35 For more information, see Outward Bound, https://www.outwardbound.org.

36 Ron Berger, "Austin's Butterfly: Models, Critique, and Descriptive Feedback," EL Education, https://www.youtube.com/watch?v=E_6PskE3zfQ.

37 See Berger, Vilen, and Woodfin, *Leaders of Their Own Learning Companion*, v.

38 Berger, Vilen, and Woodfin, 2.

39 Barron and Darling-Hammond, "Prospects and Challenges," 200.

40 Murdoch, *Power of Inquiry*, 15.

41 Murdoch, 15.

42 Murdoch, 24.

43 Murdoch, *Getting Personal With Inquiry Learning*, 23.

44 Murdoch, *Power of Inquiry*, 16.

45 Hannon and Peterson, *Thrive*, 46.

46 Hannon and Peterson, 42.

47 The EPIC (Experiential, Project Based, Indigenous, and Community) program was their source of inspiration. See EPIC: Experiential, Project-based, Indigenous, Community, https://sossepic.weebly.com.

48 See Judson, *Walking Curriculum*; see also "Walking Curriculum," imaginED, http://www.educationthatinspires.ca/walking-curriculum-imaginative-ecological -learning-activities/.

49 Strong Nations, https://www.strongnations.com.

CHAPTER 6

1 Mehta and Fine, *In Search of Deeper Learning*, 18.

2 Mehta and Fine, 15.

3 Mehta and Fine, 76.

4 Mehta and Fine, 81.

5 Kools and Stoll, "What Makes a School," 61–62.

6 Kools et al., "School as a Learning Organisation," 8.

7 Le Fevre et al., *Leading Powerful Professional Learning*, 127.

8 Earl and Timperley, *Professional Learning Conversations*.

9 Quoted in Ludwig, *Learning Tour*, 19.

10 Ludwig, *Learning Tour*, 13.

11 Ludwig, 7.

12 Ludwig, 10.

13 Ludwig, 14.

14 Ludwig, 17.

15 Williams, "Ti wa7 szwatenem. What We Know," 38.

16 Timperley et al., *Leading Professional Learning*, 61.

17 Timperley et al., 46.

18 Timperley et al., 47.

19 Timperley et al., 50.

20 See "Lead by Learning," Mills College School of Education, https://weleadbylearning.org/lead-by-learning.

21 Wilson, "Making Learning Public," 153.

22 CR4YC "is a partnership between the Ministry of Education (MOE) and the United Way of the Lower Mainland (UWLM) and was initiated in the fall of 2017." Changing Results for Young Children (CR4YC), "About CR4YC," https://cr4yr.com.

23 Drago-Severson and Blum-DeStefano, *Leading Change Together*, 25.

24 Drago-Severson and Blum-DeStefano, 20.

25 Drago-Severson and Blum-DeStefano, 28.

26 Drago-Severson and Blum-DeStefano, 29.

27 Drago-Severson and Blum-DeStefano, 28.

28 Drago-Severson and Blum-DeStefano, 31.

29 Drago-Severson and Blum-DeStefano, 32.

30 Drago-Severson and Blum-DeStefano, 22.

CHAPTER 7

1 Education Review Office | Te Tari Arotake Mātauranga, *Teaching Approaches.*

2 Timperley et al., *Leading Professional Learning*, 52.

3 Timperley et al., 55.

4 Bryk and Schneider, *Trust in Schools*, 126–27.

5 Robinson, Le Fevre, and Sinnema, *Open-to-Learning Leadership*, 234.

6 Boudett and City, *Meeting Wise*, 9–10 (original emphasis).

7 Wood, "Why Finland."

8 Wood.

9 Wood.

10 For a good description, see "About Ignite Talks," Ignite, www.ignitetalk.io/about.

11 For an introduction to the concept of teaching sprints, including testimonials and advice on how to get started, see Simon Breakspear's website, Teaching Sprints, https://teachingsprints.com/.

12 Breakspear and Jones, *Teaching Sprints*, 107.

13 This strategy has been adapted from the Critical Friends model for collegial dialogue, developed by the Annenberg Institute for School Reform at Brown University. See Storey and Richard, "The Role of Critical Friends," 415–16.

CHAPTER 8

1 Earl and Timperley, "Evaluative Thinking,"

2 Earl and Timperley, 10.

3 Le Fevre et al., *Leading Powerful Professional Learning*, 11.

4 Sahlberg, "Small Data," 19.

5 Sahlberg, 19.

6 Sahlberg, 19.

7 Safir, *Listening Leader*, 16.

8 Safir and Dugan, *Street Data*, 19.7

9 Delta School District, *District Framework.*

10 Megan Sandham, comment on Brooke Moore, "Big Three—Two Years Later," *180 Days of Learning* (blog), Delta School District, April 3, 2019, https://deltalearns.ca/180daysoflearning/2019/04/03/big-three-two-years-later.

11 McIntyre, Parveen, and Thomas, "Exclusion Rates."

12 Milligan et al., *Future-Proofing Students*, 7.

13 Milligan et al., 3.

14 "B.C. Performance Standards."

15 Milligan et al., *Future-Proofing Students*, 3.

16 Milligan et al., 4.

17 Milligan et al., 9.

18 Milligan et al., 14.

19 Milligan et al., 47.

20 See Milligan et al., Appendix 1, 47.

21 Milligan et al., 13.

22 Melbourne Graduate School of Education, "New Metrics for Success."

23 "Voice 21: Our Speaking Curriculum," School 21, https://www.school21.org.uk/voice21.

24 CASEL, Collaborative for Academic, Social and Emotional Learning, 2021, https://casel.org.

25 Student Experience Research Network (SERN), 2021, https://studentexperiencenetwork.org.

CHAPTER 9

1 Laura Curran, cited in Ludwig, *Learning Tour Study Guide*, 2.

2 Jo Chrona, "Becoming Anti-Racist in Canada: A Journey to Support Reconciliation," *Luudisk* (blog), March 11, 2021, https://luudisk.com/2021/03/11/an-anti-racist-journey/.

3 To read about the original research study, see "Indigenous Education."

4 Jana Maatoyokom Fox, personal email to authors, June 23, 2021.

5 Fox, personal communication to authors, June 23, 2021.

6 First Nations Education Steering Committee, "First Peoples Principles."

7 McGregor, Halbert, and Kaser, "Catalytic Affiliation."

8 *Delta Optimist*, "Value-Based Decisions."

9 *Delta Optimist*.

10 Kent, Sommerfeldt, and Saffer, "Social Networks, Power and Public Relations."

11 Fullan and Edwards, *Spirit Work*, xi.

12 Wheatley, foreword to *Spirit Work*, xix.

13 Battilana and Casciaro, *Power, for All*, 197.

14 The NOII NSW leadership team, started by Natalie Mansour and David Martin, expanded to include Hallie Baxter, Michael Newcombe, and Sue Sessions.

15 Sweeney, "Six Ways to Support."

16 Learn more about Story Hui on the Story Hui Trust website, https://www.storyhui.org.

17 Whole Education, home page, https://www.wholeeducation.org.

18 Whole Education, "WE Spirals of Inquiry Network," https://www.wholeeducation.org/spirals-of-inquiry-network/.

19 Netz, Nenzén, and Rehnberg, "Spirals of Inquiry."

20 "The Networks."

21 Martin Hill, "Ephemeral Sculptures: Floating Stones," 2017, https://martin-hill.com/work/ephemeral-sculptures-2/floating-stones/.

22 Kanter, *Confidence*, ch. 11.

23 For more on this subject, see Kahneman, Sibony, and Sunstein, *Noise*.

REFERENCES

Angrist, Noam, Peter Bergman, and Moitshepi Matsheng. "School's Out: Experimental Evidence on Limiting Learning Loss Using 'Low-Tech' in a Pandemic." Working Paper 28205. NBER (National Bureau of Economic Research), December 2020, revised January 2021. https://www.nber.org/papers/w28205.

Barde, Joel. "Lil'wat Nation Member Awarded Order of Canada." *Pique Newsmagazine*, January 12, 2020, https://www.piquenewsmagazine.com/sea-to-sky/lilwat-nation-member-awarded-order-of-canada-2509217.

Barron, Brigid, and Linda Darling-Hammond. "Prospects and Challenges for Inquiry-Based Approaches to Learning." In *The Nature of Learning: Using Research to Inspire Practice,* edited by Hanna Dumont, David Istance, and Francisco Benavides, 199–225. Paris: OECD, 2010.

Battilana, Julie, and Tizana Casciaro. *Power, for All: How It Really Works and Why It's Everyone's Business.* New York: Simon & Schuster, 2021.

Battiste, Marie. *Decolonizing Education: Nourishing the Learning Spirit.* Saskatoon, SK: Purich Publishing, 2015.

"B.C. Performance Standards." Department of Education and Training, Government of British Columbia, updated November 9, 2020. https://www2.gov.bc.ca/gov/content/education-training/k-12/teach/resources-for-teachers/curriculum/bc-performance-standards.

Bennett, Gavin, and Nasreen Jessani, eds. *The Knowledge Translation Toolkit: Bridging the Know-Do Gap: A Resource for Teachers.* New Delhi: Sage Publications; Ottawa: International Development Research Centre, 2011.

Berger, Ron, Leah Rugen, and Libby Woodfin. *Leaders of Their Own Learning: Transforming Schools Through Student-Engaged Assessment*. San Francisco: Jossey-Bass, 2014.

Berger, Ron, Anne Vilen, and Libby Woodfin. *The Leaders of Their Own Learning Companion: New Tools and Tips for Tackling the Common Challenges of Student-Engaged Assessment*. San Francisco: Jossey-Bass, 2020.

———. *We Are Crew: A Teamwork Approach to School Culture.* New York: EL Education, 2020.

Bishop, Russell, Mere Berryman, Sarah-Jane Tiakiwai, and Cath Richardson. *Te Kōtahitanga: The Experiences of Year 9 and 10 Māori Students in Mainstream Classrooms.* Wellington, NZ: New Zealand Ministry of Education, 2003. https://www.educationcounts.govt.nz/publications/maori/english-medium-education/9977/5375.

Black, Paul, and Dylan Wiliam. "Inside the Black Box: Raising Standards Through Classroom Assessment." *Phi Delta Kappan* 80, no. 2 (October 1998): 139–48. https://www.jstor.org/stable/20439383?refreqid=excelsior%3Af642107937a6a605b713768494e53186

Boaler, Jo. *Limitless Mind: Learn, Lead, and Live Without Barriers.* New York: HarperOne, 2019.

Boekaerts, Monique. "The Crucial Role of Motivation and Emotion in Classroom Learning." In *The Nature of Learning: Using Research to Inspire Practice*, edited by Hanna Dumont, David Istance, and Francisco Benavides, 91–111. Paris: OECD, 2010.

Boudett, Kathryn Parker, and Elizabeth A. City. *Meeting Wise: Making the Most of Collaborative Time for Educators*. Cambridge, MA: Harvard Education Press, 2014.

Breakspear, Simon, and Bronwyn Ryrie Jones. *Teaching Sprints: How Overworked Educators Can Keep Getting Better*. Thousand Oaks, CA: Corwin, 2021.

British Columbia Ministry of Education. *Aboriginal Worldviews and Perspectives in the Classroom: Moving Forward*. Victoria, BC: Queen's Printer for British Columbia, 2015. https://www2.gov.bc.ca/assets/gov/education/administration/kindergarten-to-grade-12/indigenous-education/awp_moving_forward.pdf.

Brown, Brené. *Daring Greatly: How the Courage to Be Vulnerable Transforms the Way We Live, Love, Parent, and Lead*. New York: Penguin Random House, 2015.

Bryk, Anthony S., and Barbara Schneider. *Trust in Schools: A Core Resource for School Reform*. New York: Russell Sage Foundation, 2003.

Butler, Deborah L., Leyton Schnellert, and Nancy E. Perry. *Developing Self-Regulating Learners*. Toronto: Pearson Canada, 2017.

Chrona, Jo. *Wayi Wah! Indigenous Pedagogies: An Act for Reconciliation and Anti-Racist Education*. Winnipeg, MB: Portage & Main Press, 2022 [in press].

Clarke, Paul. *Education for Sustainability: Becoming Naturally Smart*. New York: Routledge, 2012.

Dalton, Joan. *Learning Talk: Important Conversations at Work*. Maldon, AU: Leading Adult Learners, 2016.

Daly, Alan J., and Louise Stoll. "Looking Back and Moving Forward: Where to Next for Networks of Learning?" In *Networks for Learning: Effective Collaboration for Teacher, School and System Improvement*, edited by Chris Brown and Cindy L. Poortman, 205–13. New York: Routledge, 2018.

Delta Optimist. "Value-Based Decisions Lead to Community Action." April 2, 2021, https://www.delta-optimist.com/in-the-community/value-based-decisions-lead-to-community-action-3597768.

Delta School District, British Columbia. *District Framework for Enhancing Student Learning, 2018–2021*. Infographic. British Columbia: Delta School District, April 2018. https://www.deltasd.bc.ca/wp-content/uploads/sites/2/2018/04/DSDInfographic_Final_DIGITAL.pdf.

Douglas, Brooke, and Brooke Moore. "Guiding Growth and Change: How Two Made-In-BC Protocols Can Help Forge a Path Through Tough Conversations." *Principl(ed)*, June 2021. https://bcpvpa.insite.com/files/assets/563/principl-ed-june2021-forweb.pdf.

Drago-Severson, Eleanor, and Jessica Blum-DeStefano. *Leading Change Together: Developing Educator Capacity Within Schools and Systems*. Alexandria, VA: ASCD, 2018.

Dumont, Hanna, David Istance, and Francisco Benavides, eds. *The Nature of Learning: Using Research to Inspire Practice*. Paris: OECD, 2010. https://read.oecd-ilibrary.org/education/the-nature-of-learning_9789264086487-en#page1.

Dumont, Hanna, David Istance, and Francisco Benavides, eds. *The Nature of Learning: Using Research to Inspire Practice: Practitioner's Guide*. Prepared by Jennifer Groff. Paris: OECD, 2012. https://www.oecd.org/education/ceri/50300814.pdf.

Dweck, Carol S. *The New Psychology of Success*. New York: Random House, 2006.

Earl, Lorna M. *Assessment As Learning: Using Classroom Assessment to Maximize Student Learning*. 2nd ed. Thousand Oaks, CA: Corwin, 2013.

Earl, Lorna M., and Helen Timperley. "Evaluative Thinking for Successful Educational Innovation." OECD Education Working Papers Series 122. OECD, July 2015. https://doi.org/10.1787/5jrxtk1jtdwf-en.

———. *Professional Learning Conversations: Challenges in Using Evidence for Improvement*. Professional Learning and Development in Schools and Higher Education 1. Dordrecht, NL: Springer, 2008.

Education Review Office | Te Tari Arotake Mātauranga. *Teaching Approaches and Strategies That Work: Keeping Children Engaged and Achieving in the Upper Primary School*. Education Review Office of the New Zealand Government, November 2017. https://ero.govt.nz/our-research/teaching-approaches-and-strategies-that-work.

Egan, Kieran. *Learning in Depth: A Simple Innovation That Can Transform Schooling*. Chicago: University of Chicago Press, 2011.

Engel, Susan. *The Hungry Mind: The Origins of Curiosity in Childhood*. Cambridge, MA: Harvard University Press, 2015.

Failing, Lee, Robin Gregory, Graham Long, and Brooke Moore. *The Decision Playbook: Making Thoughtful Choices in a Complex World*. Teacher's ed. Vancouver: GutsNHeads Project, 2019. https://www.deltalearns.ca/decisions/the-decision-playbook/.

First Nations Education Steering Committee (FNESC). "First Peoples Principles of Learning." 2008. http://www.fnesc.ca/first-peoples-principles-of-learning/.

Fryberg, Stephanie A., Rebecca Covarrubias, and Jacob A. Burack. "The Ongoing Psychological Colonization of North American Indigenous People: Using Social Psychological Theories to Promote Social Justice." In *Oxford Handbook of Social Psychology and Social Justice*, edited by Phillip L. Hammack, 113–28. New York: Oxford University Press, 2018.

Fullan, Michael. *Stratosphere: Integrating Technology, Pedagogy and Change Knowledge*. Toronto: Pearson Canada, 2012.

Fullan, Michael, and Mark Edwards. *Spirit Work and the Science of Collaboration*. Thousand Oaks, CA: Corwin Sage, 2022.

Goodwin, Bryan. *Building a Curious School: Restore the Joy That Brought You to School*. Thousand Oaks, CA: Corwin; Denver: McRel International, 2020.

Grant, Adam. *Think Again: The Power of Knowing What You Don't Know*. New York: Viking, 2021.

Halbert, Judy, and Linda Kaser. *Spirals of Inquiry: For Equity and Quality*. Vancouver: BC Principals' and Vice-Principals' Association (BCPVPA), 2013.

Hannon, Valerie, and Amelia Peterson. *Thrive: The Purpose of Schools in a Changing World*. Cambridge, UK: Cambridge University Press, 2021.

Hargreaves, Andy, and Dennis Shirley. *Well-Being in Schools: Three Forces That Will Uplift Your Students in a Volatile World*. Alexandria, VA: ASCD, 2021.

Hatano, Giyoo, and Kayoko Inagaki. "Two Courses of Expertise." In *Child Development and Education in Japan*, edited by Harold Stevenson, Hiroshi Azuma, and Kenji Hakuta, 262–72. New York: Freeman, 1986.

Hattie, John, and Helen Timperley. "The Power of Feedback." *Review of Educational Research* 77, no. 1 (March 2007): 81–112. https://doi.org/10.3102/003465430298487.

Healey, Kaleen, and Chloe Stroman. "Structures for Belonging: A Synthesis of Research on Belonging-Supportive Learning Environments." Center to Improve Social and Emotional Learning and School Safety, WestEd, 2021. https://selcenter.wested.org/resource/structures-for-belonging-a-synthesis-of-research-on-belonging-supportive-learning-environments/#.

"Indigenous Education." Networks of Inquiry and Indigenous Education (NOIIE). 2021. https://noiie.ca/indigenous/.

Istance, David, and Hannah Dumont. "Future Directions for Learning Environments in the 21st Century." In *The Nature of Learning: Using Research to Inspire Practice*, edited by Hannah Dumont, David Istance, and Francisco Benavides, 319–27. Paris: OECD, 2010.

James, Carrie, Emily Weinstein, and Kelly Mendoza. *Teaching Digital Citizens in Today's World: Research and Insights Behind the Common Sense Digital Citizenship Curriculum*. Version 2. San Francisco, CA: Common Sense Media, 2021. https://d1e2bohyu2u2w9.cloudfront.net/education/sites/default/files/tlr_component/common_sense_education_digital_citizenship_research_backgrounder.pdf.

Jensen, Ben, Julie Sonnemann, Katie Roberts-Hull, and Amélie Hunter. *Beyond PD: Teacher Professional Learning in High-Performing Systems*. Washington, DC: National Center on Education and the Economy (NCEE), 2016.

Judson, Gillian. *A Walking Curriculum: Evoking a Sense of Wonder and Developing Sense of Place (K–12)*. Middletown, DE: Self-published, 2018.

Kahneman, Daniel. *Thinking, Fast and Slow*. New York: Farrar, Straus and Giroux, 2011.

Kahneman, Daniel, Olivier Sibony, and Cass R. Sunstein. *Noise: A Flaw in Human Judgment*. New York: Little, Brown Spark, 2021.

Kanter, Rosabeth Moss. *Confidence: How Winning Streaks and Losing Streaks Begin and End*. New York: Three Rivers, 2006.

Kaser, Linda, and Judy Halbert. "A Cross-Grade Learner Conversation." In *Professional Learning Conversations: Challenges in Using Evidence for Improvement*, edited by Lorna M. Earl and Helen Timperley, 53–68. London: Springer, 2009.

———. *Leadership Mindsets: Innovation and Learning in the Transformation of Schools*. London: Routledge, 2009.

———. *The Spiral Playbook: Leading With an Inquiring Mindset in School Systems and Schools*. Toronto: C21 Canada, 2017.

Keene, Ellin Oliver, and Susan Zimmerman. *Mosaic of Thought: The Power of Comprehension Strategy Instruction*. 2nd ed. Portsmouth, NH: Heinemann, 2007.

Kent, Michael, Erich J. Sommerfeldt, and Adam J. Saffer. "Social Networks, Power, and Public Relations: *Tertius Iungens* as a Cocreational Approach to Studying Relationship Networks." *Public Relations Review* 42, no. 1 (March 2016): 91–100. https://doi.org/10.1016/j.pubrev.2015.08.002.

Kimmerer, Robin Wall. *Braiding Sweetgrass: Indigenous Wisdom, Scientific Knowledge, and the Teaching of Plants*. Minneapolis, MN: Milkweed Editions, 2013.

Kools, Marco, and Louise Stoll. "What Makes a School a Learning Organisation?" OECD Education Working Papers 137. OECD, July 2016. https://doi.org/10.1787/5jlwm62b3bvh-en.

Kools, Marco, Louise Stoll, Bert George, Bram Steijn, Victo Bekkers, and Pierre Gouëdard. "The School as a Learning Organisation: The Concept and Its Measurement." *European Journal of Education* (March 2020): 1–19. https://www.researchgate.net/publication/338810180_The_school_as_a_learning_organisation_The_concept_and_its_measurement.

Le Fevre, Deidre M., Viviane M. J. Robinson, and Claire E. L. Sinnema. "Genuine Inquiry: Widely Espoused Yet Rarely Enacted." *Educational Management, Administration and Leadership* 43, no. 6 (November 2015): 883–99. https://doi.org/10.1177%2F1741143214543204.

Le Fevre, Deirdre M., Helen Timperley, Kaye Twyford, and Fiona Ell. *Leading Powerful Professional Learning: Responding to Complexity With Adaptive Expertise*. Thousand Oaks, CA: Corwin, 2019; Oxford, OH: Learning Forward, 2020.

Lucas, Bill. *Rethinking Assessment in Education: The Case for Change*. Centre for Strategic Education Leading Education Series. Melbourne: Centre for Strategic Education, 2021

Ludwig, Catherine. *Learning Tour Study Guide*. Vancouver: Networks of Inquiry and Indigenous Education (NOIIE), 2021. https://noiie.ca/wp-content/uploads/2021/03/Study-Guide_single-pages_WEB.pdf.

MacDonald, Barry. *Boy Smarts: Mentoring Boys for Success at School*. Surrey, BC: Mentoring Boys, 2005.

Macintosh, Joanna, Manjot Kandola, Ying Yin Lei, Anushka Talwar, Jaeda Schilke, and Devansh Vasudev. "Transforming the Vice-Principal's Office: Leading and Learning Through Collaborative Inquiry with Students." *Transformative Educational Leadership (TEL) Journal* (November 2020). https://teljournal.educ.ubc.ca/2020/11/transforming-the-vice-principals-office-leading-and-learning-through-collaborative-inquiry-with-students/.

McGregor, Catherine, Judy Halbert, and Linda Kaser. "Catalytic Affiliation: Theoretical and Practical Implications for Professional Learning Networks." Paper presented at International Congress for School Effectiveness and Improvement (ICSEI) Virtual Congress, January 6, 2022.

McIntyre, Niamh, Nazia Parveen, and Tobi Thomas. "Exclusion Rates Five Times Higher for Black Caribbean Pupils in Parts of England." *The Guardian*, March 24, 2021. https://www.theguardian.com/education/2021/mar/24/exclusion-rates-black-caribbean-pupils-england.

Mehta, Jal, and Sarah Fine. *In Search of Deeper Learning: The Quest to Remake the American High School*. Cambridge, MA: Harvard University Press, 2019.

Melbourne Graduate School of Education. "New Metrics for Success: Transforming What We Value in Schools." Melbourne: University of Melbourne, Melbourne Graduate School of Education, updated 2021. https://education.unimelb.edu.au/new-metrics-for-success.

Milligan, Sandra, Rebekah Luo, Eeqbal Hassim, and Jayne Johnston. Executive Summary of *Future-Proofing Students: What They Need to Know and How Educators Can Assess and Credential Them*. Melbourne: University of Melbourne, Melbourne Graduate School of Education, 2020. https://education.unimelb.edu.au/mgse-industry-reports/report-2-future-proofing-students.

———. *Future-Proofing Students: What They Need to Know and How Educators Can Assess and Credential Them*. Melbourne: University of Melbourne, Melbourne Graduate School of Education, 2020. https://all-learning.org.au/app/uploads/2020/12/MGSE_Future-Proofing-Students_Web_Updated-9-7-20.pdf.

Moore, Brooke. *Spiral of Inquiry and Decision-Maker Moves: A Rigorous Blend*. Discussion paper. Networks of Inquiry and Indigenous Education (NOIIE) and Delta School District, BC, June 2020. https://noiie.ca/wp-content/uploads/2020/09/Spiral-Decisions.pdf.

Murdoch, Kath. *Getting Personal With Inquiry Learning: A Practical Guide to Working With Young Learners' Questions, Passions, Interests and the Issues That Matter to Them*. Vancouver: Seastar Education, 2022 [in press].

———. *The Power of Inquiry: Teaching and Learning With Curiosity, Creativity, and Purpose in the Contemporary Classroom*. Northcote, AU: Seastar Education, 2015.

Murphy, Mark. "HARD Goals, Not SMART Goals, Are the Key to Career Development." *Forbes*, June 11, 2017. https:/www.forbes.com/sites/markmurphy/2017/06/11/hard-goals-not-smart-goals-are-the-key-to-career-development/?sh=99dadb570fb4.

"The Networks: Deepening Learning Through Inquiry, Innovation, and Teamwork." Networks of Inquiry and Indigenous Education (NOIIE), January 13, 2021. https://noiie.ca/about-us/.

Netz, Ingela, Margareta Nenzén, and Lillemor Rehnberg. "Spirals of Inquiry: Bringing Meaning to Work in Swedish Schools and Municipalities." *Transformative Educational Leadership (TEL) Journal* (April 2020). https://teljournal.educ.ubc.ca/2020/04/spirals-of-inquiry-bringing-meaning-to-work-in-swedish-schools-and-municipalities/.

Nolen, Susan Bobbitt, Christopher J. Ward, and Ilana Seidel Horn. "Motivation, Engagement, and Identity: Opening a Conversation." In *Sociocultural Theories of Learning and Motivation: Looking Back, Looking Forward*, edited by Dennis M. McInerney, Richard A. Walker, and Gregory Arief D. Liem, 109–35. Vol. 10 of *Research on Sociocultural Influences on Motivation and Learning*. Charlotte, NC: Information Age Publishing, 2011.

Nottingham, James, and Bosse Larsson. *Challenging Mindset: Why a Growth Mindset Makes a Difference in Learning—and What to Do When It Doesn't*. Challenging Learning. Thousand Oaks, CA: Corwin, 2019.

Organisation for Economic Co-operation and Development (OECD). "The Future of Education and Skills: Education 2030." Position Paper, Directorate for Education and Skills, OECD, May 2018. https://www.oecd.org/education/2030-project/about /documents/E2030%20Position%20Paper%20(05.04.2018).pdf.

Perez, Kathy. *The Social-Emotional Learning Toolbox: Practical Strategies to Support All Students*. Baltimore: Paul H. Brookes, 2022.

Pfeffer, Jeffrey, and Robert I. Sutton. *The Knowing-Doing Gap: How Smart Companies Turn Knowledge Into Action*. Boston: Harvard Business School Press, 2000.

Ritchhart, Ron, and Mark Church. *The Power of Making Thinking Visible: Practices to Engage and Empower All Learners*. Hoboken, NJ: Jossey-Bass, 2020.

Ritchhart, Ron, Mark Church, and Karen Morrison. *Making Thinking Visible: How to Promote Engagement, Understanding, and Independence for All Learners*. San Francisco: Jossey-Bass, 2011.

Robinson, Viviane M. J., Deirdre Le Fevre, and Claire Sinnema. *Open-to-Learning Leadership: How to Build Trust While Tackling Tough Issues*. Melbourne: Bastow Institute of Educational Leadership, 2016.

Robinson, Viviane M. J., Frauke Meyer, Deidre Le Fevre, and Claire Sinnema. "The Quality of Leaders' Problem-Solving Conversations: Truth-Seeking or Truth-Claiming?" *Leadership and Policy in Schools* 20, no. 4 (March 2020): 650–71. https://doi.org/10.1080/15700763.2020.1734627.

Safir, Shane. *The Listening Leader: Creating the Conditions for Equitable School Transformation*. San Francisco: Jossey-Bass, 2017.

Safir, Shane, and Jamila Dugan. *Street Data: A Next Generation Model for Equity, Pedagogy and School Transformation*. Thousand Oaks, CA: Corwin, 2021.

Sahlberg, Pasi. "Small Data for Big Change: What Does It Mean for Teachers?" *ATA Magazine* (May 2017): 18–20. https://pasisahlberg.com/wp-content/uploads/2017/08/ATA-Small-Data-2017-1.pdf.

Sinek, Simon. *The Infinite Game*. New York: Portfolio, 2019.

———. *Start With Why: How Great Leaders Inspire Everyone to Take Action*. New York: Portfolio, 2009.

Stoll, Louise, and Julie Temperley. "Narrowing the Gap with Spirals of Enquiry: Evaluation of Whole Education's Pilot." Discussion paper. Whole Education, November 2015. https://1stdirectory.co.uk/_assets/files_comp/e8306235-a4ab-4680-835a-edfae27833c1.pdf.

Storey, Valerie A., and Brendan Richard. "The Role of Critical Friends in Supporting Institutional Change." *Journal of Applied Research in Higher Education* 7, no. 2 (September 2015): 412–28. http://dx.doi.org/10.1108/JARHE-10-2013-0043.

Sweeney, Rebbecca. "Six Ways to Support the Implementation of the Spiral of Inquiry: Lessons from New Zealand." *Transformative Educational Leadership (TEL) Journal* (April 2020). https://teljournal.educ.ubc.ca/2020/04/spiral-of-inquiry-lessons-from-new-zealand/.

Tilleczek, Kate. "Building Bridges: Transitions from Elementary to Secondary School." *Education Canada* 48, no. 1 (2008): 68–71. https://www.edcan.ca/wp-content/uploads/EdCan-2008-v48-n1-Tilleczek.pdf.

Timperley, Helen, Fiona Ell, Deidre Le Fevre, and Kaye Twyford. *Leading Professional Learning: Practical Strategies for Impact in Schools*. Melbourne, AU: ACER, 2020.

Timperley, Helen, Linda Kaser, and Judy Halbert. "A Framework for Transforming Learning in Schools: Innovation and the Spiral of Inquiry." CSE Seminar Series Paper 234, Centre for Strategic Education, April 2014. https://www.exeterconsortium.com/uploads/1/1/5/9/115936395/innovationandthespiralofinquiry.pdf.

Timperley, Helen, Aaron Wilson, Heather Barrar, and Irene Fung. *Teacher Professional Learning and Development: Best Evidence Synthesis (BES)*. Wellington, NZ: Government of New Zealand, 2007. https://www.educationcounts.govt.nz/publications/series/2515/15341.

Twyford, Kaye, and Deidre Le Fevre. "Leadership, Uncertainty and Risk: How Leaders Influence Teachers." *Journal of Professional Capital and Community* 4, no. 4 (August 2019): 309–24. https://doi.org/10.1108/JPCC-02-2019-0002.

Valiente, Carlos, Jodi Swanson, and Nancy Eisenberg. "Linking Students' Emotions and Academic Achievement: When and Why Emotions Matter." *Child Development Perspectives* 6, no. 2 (June 2012): 129–35. https://www.ncbi.nlm.nih.gov/pmc/articles/PMC3482624/.

Walsh, Bari. "The Science of Resilience: Why Some Children Can Thrive Despite Adversity." Usable Knowledge: Relevant Research for Today's Researchers. Harvard Graduate School of Education, March 23, 2015. https://www.gse.harvard.edu/news/uk/15/03/science-resilience.

Watkins, John, Amelia Peterson, and Jal Mehta. 2018. "Transforming School Districts to Support Deeper Learning for All: A Hypothesis." White paper. Deeper Learning Dozen, October 2018. https://static1.squarespace.com/static/5bae5a3492441bf2930bacd1/t/5c044d39758d469484888c20/1543786237346/Deeper+Learning+Dozen+White+Paper+%28Public+2%29.pdf.

Wheatley, Margaret J. Foreword to *Spirit Work and the Science of Collaboration*, edited by Michael Fullan and Mark Edwards, xi–xv. Thousand Oaks, CA: Corwin Sage, 2022.

White, Katie. *Softening the Edges: Assessment Practices That Honor K–12 Teachers and Learners*. Bloomington, IN: Solution Tree, 2017.

———. *Unlocked: Assessment as the Key to Everyday Creativity in the Classroom*. Bloomington, IN: Solution Tree, 2019.

Wiliam, Dylan, and Siobhán Leahy. *Embedding Formative Assessment: Practical Techniques for K–12 Classrooms*. West Palm Beach, FL: Learning Sciences International, 2015.

Williams, Lorna. "Ti wa7 szwatenem. What We Know: Indigenous Knowledge and Learning." *BC Studies* 200 (Winter 2018/19): 31–44. https://doi.org/10.14288/bcs.v0i200.191456.

Wilson, Carrie. "Making Learning Public: Valuing Teachers' Voices." In *Street Data*, edited by Shane Safir and Jamila Dugan, 147–65. Thousand Oaks, CA: Corwin, 2021.

Winthrop, Rebecca, Adam Barton, Mahsa Ershadi, and Lauren Ziegler. *Collaborating to Transform and Improve Education Systems*. Washington, DC: Brookings Institution, 2021.

Winthrop, Rebecca, Adam Barton, and Eileen McGivney. *Leapfrogging Inequality: Remaking Education to Help Young People Thrive*. Washington, DC: Brookings Institution, 2018.

Wood, Heidi, and Gillian Judson. "Walking Forward: Walking With a First Peoples Focus; Making Connections to the Walking Curriculum." Walking Forward, 2019. https://walkingforwardfp.weebly.com.

Wood, Jessica. "Why Finland Has a National Day of Failure." *Culture Trip*, October 3, 2017, https://theculturetrip.com/europe/finland/articles/why-finland-has-a-national-day-of-failure/.